I0531185

PEACE ON DEMAND

MASTER YOUR MIND, CONTROL YOUR WORLD

JAMIL JOINTER

DEDICATION

For my grandmother, Peggy Love, who taught me to always be watchful, cautious, and prepared. Your constant concern for those you loved showed me the importance of vigilance. What you carried as worry, I now carry forward as discipline and protection. This book is a reflection of that legacy.

To my family, who gave me purpose. To every warrior who seeks clarity and discipline in a chaotic world.

CONTENTS

Chapter 1: Discipline as the Foundation 1

Chapter 2: The Brain's Blueprint: How Habits Shape Reality 20

Chapter 3: Discipline in Action 33

Chapter 4: Mastering Emotional Independence:
            Becoming the Anchor in Any Storm........................64

Chapter 5: The Power of Decision-Making: Leading
            with Clarity Under Pressure....................................84

Chapter 6: Strategic Vision and Execution: Turning
            Ideas into Reality. 106

Chapter 7: The Lone Wolf Advantage: Self-Reliance as
            the First Step to Leadership 126

Chapter 8: Battling the Desires of the Flesh: Discipline
            Over Impulse 149

Chapter 9: Nutrition for the Mind and Body: Fueling
            Discipline and Clarity..166

Chapter 10: The Five-Day Fast: Training the Will
            Through Sacrifice..179

Chapter 11: Your Personal Navigation System: Daily and
            Long-Term Application Plan 189

Discipline as the Foundation

Discipline Over Motivation

The alarm blares, an unwelcome sound before dawn breaks. The warmth of the bed feels like a sanctuary, and every muscle in your body protests, urging you to stay nestled in the comfort of sleep. The cold air outside feels like a challenge, a reminder of the responsibility awaiting you. And inside, the weight of the day's tasks presses down harder than any physical fatigue. Your mind scrambles for reasons to stay in the comfort of sleep, to delay what lies ahead.

In these moments, motivation is nowhere to be found. The enthusiasm that once fueled your drive has vanished. The so-called "spark" that many chase after has either fizzled out or hasn't arrived at all. The fire that motivates you to act, the energy that makes you feel like you can conquer the world, seems absent.

Yet, amidst all this, something far stronger and more dependable moves you forward: DISCIPLINE. Discipline is not a fleeting emotion; it is a conscious decision, a contract you made with yourself long before the alarm went off. It's the promise to show up, to take action, and to perform, regardless of how you feel in the moment.

Unlike motivation, which ebbs and flows, discipline is steady and constant. It is the decision to act, even when you feel uninspired, fatigued, or overwhelmed by the day ahead.

Discipline doesn't care about your mood. It doesn't care if you're tired, stressed, or lacking inspiration. It is the force that keeps you grounded, that propels you into action even when all you want to do is retreat. While motivation may show up on a good day, discipline is always present. It's your internal guide when motivation falters.

The truth is that most people chase motivation endlessly. They look for external triggers like quotes, playlists, speeches, or a sudden rush of energy to spark their momentum. They believe that the key to success lies in finding the right source of motivation. But this is where the irony lies. Motivation, though helpful in short bursts, is inherently unreliable. It burns brightly but flickers out quickly. Once the initial enthusiasm wanes, it leaves you with nothing but the aftermath of a temporary high. On the other hand, discipline remains unshaken. It's the steady hand that steers the ship through rough seas, the force that keeps you going even when the wind and rain threaten to derail you.

Discipline is the driving force that converts repeated, often mundane, actions into long-term results. It's what turns consistent effort into meaningful progress. While motivation comes and goes like a gust of wind, discipline is the steady current beneath the surface, guiding you toward your destination. Without discipline, opportunities slip away unnoticed, as you are constantly waiting for the perfect conditions to act. But with discipline, every action, no matter how small, compounds and builds momentum. Over time, this momentum creates credibility, trust, and mastery. Discipline is what shapes your character, your actions, and ultimately, your success.

Think about it: discipline doesn't just happen. It's not a skill you learn overnight. It's built through small, repetitive actions that you choose to take, regardless of how you feel. The more you commit to these actions, the more your discipline becomes ingrained. It becomes a part of who you are, and as it grows, it makes you resilient. When challenges arise, as they inevitably do, you won't rely on motivation to get through. You'll rely on the system you've built on your discipline. Motivation is a fleeting visitor that may light the path, but discipline is the force that keeps you moving forward day after day.

Most people think success comes from having bursts of motivation. But true success comes from being able to act consistently, regardless of your emotional state. Motivation may help you get started, but discipline is what keeps you going. Without it, your efforts will falter. With it, you will experience sustained progress, building momentum, credibility, and mastery over time.

In short: motivation is temporary, but discipline is permanent. It's the resident force in your life, the one that drives long-term success. Motivation will come and go, but discipline? It will stay. And once you've made it your default setting, everything else will follow.

Why Discipline Is Non-Negotiable

Motivation feels electric, it ignites action, makes you sprint toward goals with energy and excitement. But the fire fades. Motivation is unreliable. It starts you, but it cannot carry you through the grind.

Discipline, in contrast, is durable, steady, and unshaken by fleeting emotions. It is the muscle that persists when the spark fades, when the alarm rings, or when the path grows difficult. Bills arrive, teams expect results, and life does not wait for your enthusiasm. Only discipline ensures that you show up, keep commitments, and maintain consistency over time.

The gap between desire and reality is wide. Everyone wants success, health, financial stability, and meaningful relationships. But desire alone is fragile. It collapses under pressure. Discipline is the bridge that converts intention into action, day after day.

Examples in Practice:

- Entrepreneur: The business owner who thrives is not the one who waits for inspiration but the one who practices daily discipline; tracking numbers, reaching out to clients, and refining systems consistently.
- Athlete: Talent wins games, but discipline wins championships. Training only when motivated leaves gaps; consistent practice builds stamina, skill, and resilience.
- Parent: Children require consistency regardless of mood. Parents who show up daily with guidance, structure, and care model discipline that shapes long-term stability.

Discipline Builds Trust:

At its core, discipline builds trust. People trust those who are consistent. A team trusts a leader who always shows up. A partner trusts someone who keeps their word. Even within ourselves, trust is built the same way when we keep promises to ourselves. Through discipline, our confidence grows, when we break those promises, our self-trust erodes.

That is why discipline is non-negotiable. Without it, life becomes a series of broken promises, excuses, and half-finished goals. With it, you develop a reputation for others and for yourself as someone who can be relied upon.

The Three Levels of Discipline

Discipline is not a single act; it is a layered system that grows in depth and scope. Each layer supports the next, forming a foundation for personal mastery, operational excellence, and strategic vision. Understanding these levels ensures that discipline is not random effort but a coherent framework for life and leadership.

Level One: Personal Discipline (Mastering the Self)

The first layer is *personal discipline*: the decisions you make when no one is watching. Personal discipline includes habits like:

- Waking up on time consistently
- Maintaining health and fitness routines
- Keeping commitments to yourself and others
- Managing finances responsibly

Example: A professional struggles to maintain a consistent morning routine. By placing the alarm across the room and preparing gear the night before, they gradually build the habit of showing up on time. This small change strengthens self-respect and sets the tone for larger commitments.

Level Two: Operational Discipline (Strength in Systems)

The second layer is *operational discipline*: It means how your personal discipline scales within systems, teams, or organizations. Even a highly disciplined individual can fail if their systems are inconsistent or unstructured. Operational discipline includes:

- Maintaining routines and procedures
- Communicating clearly within teams
- Creating accountability structures

Example: A business delivers reliably because its systems work, orders are shipped on time, client communication is prompt, and errors are addressed systematically. In a military setting, operational discipline ensures units coordinate effectively under pressure.

Level Three: Strategic Discipline (Loyalty to Vision)

The highest layer is strategic discipline: unwavering commitment to long-term vision and core principles. This is what keeps leaders aligned when short-term temptations threaten to divert focus. Strategic discipline ensures:

- Decisions reflect values, not impulses
- Visionary goals guide daily actions
- Short-term sacrifices serve long-term outcomes

Example: Leaders pressured to bend rules for immediate gains who remain loyal to their principles earn enduring respect and credibility. Strategic discipline may require patience, but it ensures legacy and trust.

Discipline as a Shield Against Chaos

Life guarantees disruption. No matter how carefully we plan, chaos will arrive; unexpected financial setbacks, health crises, leadership challenges, or sudden changes in circumstances. In these moments, talent, charm, and even motivation often fail. What holds the line is discipline. It is the shield that keeps you grounded when the storm tears through every other defense.

Chaos in Leadership

Leaders frequently face uncertainty. A project may fail, a team member might under-perform, or an urgent decision could demand attention. Without discipline, reactions become emotional; shifting strategies hourly, overreacting, or withdrawing entirely. Discipline allows leaders to absorb the chaos.

Chaos at Home

Chaos is not confined to the professional arena. Families experience disruptions too such as unexpected bills, emergencies, or changes in routine. A disciplined household absorbs the shock better. Predictable routines, savings habits, and open communication create resilience. While stress exists, it doesn't overwhelm, because disciplined systems act as shock absorbers.

Chaos Within Yourself

Internal chaos; anxiety, anger, or fear can cloud judgment. Discipline acts as a stabilizer. Techniques like journaling, deep breathing, and pre-decided routines create "muscle memory" for the mind, ensuring clarity even under pressure.

Core Lesson

Chaos cannot be avoided, but collapse can. Discipline doesn't eliminate storms; it shields you so you can stand firm. Systems, routines, and habits are survival tools when everything breaks. The disciplined individual becomes unshakable not because life is easier, but because they are prepared for its hardest moments.

Discipline, Pain & Growth

Discipline is forged in discomfort. Growth rarely occurs in comfort zones, it is cultivated in tension, repetition, and the moments we choose action over ease. Pain, when approached with purpose, becomes the forge where resilience and discipline harden.

The Principle of Purposeful Discomfort

Life is filled with situations that challenge us physically, mentally, and emotionally. Without discomfort, there is no adaptation. When approached intentionally, each moment of pain is a signal; a training ground for the mind and spirit.

Composite Example:

- Military recruits face exhausting drills, pushing beyond perceived limits to build endurance.
- Athletes train through fatigue, learning their bodies can sustain far more than their minds initially believe.
- Working parents manage long days, early mornings, and relentless responsibility, discovering strength in consistent effort.

In all cases, discomfort is a teacher. Discipline turns resistance into growth, endurance into mastery, and pain into fuel for long-term achievement.

The Transformation of Pain into Progress

- Physical Pain: Regular exposure to controlled physical stress through exercise, endurance challenges, or disciplined movement trains both body and mind to respond calmly under strain.
- Emotional Pain: Facing difficult conversations, setbacks, or fears strengthens emotional resilience. The disciplined individual learns to act despite fear or frustration.
- Mental Pain: Tackling challenging problems, enduring boredom, or working without immediate reward strengthens focus and patience.

Principle: Pain with Purpose

Suffering without direction is wasted energy. Discipline gives pain purpose: it becomes the measure of growth rather than a barrier. Every uncomfortable choice completed intentionally strengthens habits, reinforces self-control, and expands capacity.

Discipline, Resilience, and Leadership

Enduring discomfort consistently builds trust; both internally and externally. People follow leaders who can stand steady under pressure. Families, teams, and communities feel confidence when they see resilience modeled consistently. Pain becomes a tool for credibility, stability, and influence.

By integrating purposeful discomfort into your daily structure, you create a bridge from ordinary action to extraordinary outcomes. The challenges of life no longer dictate your response; discipline shapes your action.

Leadership & Discipline

Discipline is the foundation of effective leadership. It is what provides predictability, stability, and credibility in any environment, military, business, or personal. Leadership is not about charisma or loud declarations; it is about consistency, reliability, and the ability to act deliberately even under pressure.

People trust leaders who consistently show up and follow through on commitments. Discipline communicates reliability: it tells your team, family, or community that they can depend on you. Trust, once earned through consistent action, creates influence without the need for force or persuasion.

A disciplined leader approaches decision with clarity, structure, and patience. They do not react impulsively to every crisis, temptation, or trend. Instead, they rely on pre-established systems and principles to guide action.

Leading by Example

Discipline extends beyond personal action—it sets the standard for others. The most effective leaders demonstrate the behaviors they expect from their team. When routines, commitments, and values are modeled consistently, others internalize and emulate them.

Example: A team leader arrives early, completes daily planning, and checks follow-ups consistently. Team members, witnessing this, adopt similar habits without explicit instruction.

The Challenge of Leadership Discipline

The challenge for any leader is to consistently model discipline, even when the world around them seems chaotic. Whether leading a team, a family, or a community, the most trusted leaders are those who stay steady, even when times are tough.

Discipline = Freedom

The Paradox of Discipline = Freedom

At first glance, discipline may seem like a restriction. It involves tough choices, delayed gratification, and resisting temptations. But in truth, discipline is the key that unlocks freedom. Discipline is not about limiting your options, it's about creating space for what truly matters. It gives you clarity, control, and the ability to make decisions without the overwhelming weight of distractions and uncertainty.

Freedom Through Structure

The common misconception is that discipline limits freedom. In fact, discipline creates structure, and structure is what leads to freedom. When your routines, goals, and time are organized through discipline, you no longer waste precious mental energy on deciding what to do next. You're not at the mercy of your impulses. Instead, you are empowered to focus on your most important priorities.

For example, imagine starting your day with a consistent morning routine: waking up at the same time, meditating, exercising, and planning your day. Rather than feeling rushed and chaotic, you begin the day with intention and energy. This disciplined approach frees up mental bandwidth, allowing you to be more productive and focused throughout the day.

Freedom from Guilt and Anxiety

Discipline also frees you from guilt and anxiety. Think about how often you've felt stressed because you weren't sticking to a plan or achieving your goals. This mental clutter weighs you down. But when you live with discipline whether in health, work, or finances you remove this burden.

For example, a person who practices financial discipline like budgeting, saving, and investing doesn't worry about money in the same way as someone who lives paycheck to paycheck. Financial discipline gives them the freedom to make bigger, life-changing decisions without the constant stress of debt or insecurity.

Discipline = Financial Freedom

One of the most profound ways discipline leads to freedom is through financial independence. The temptation to overspend or avoid difficult financial choices is strong, but these habits create financial bondage. In contrast, when you practice financial discipline like budgeting, saving, and investing you break free from the cycle of debt and financial stress. This discipline secures your present and gives you the freedom to shape your future.

The Bigger Picture: The Freedom to Choose

Discipline gives you the freedom to choose. Without it, your options are limited by external chaos or internal struggles. With discipline, you create your own path, shaping your life on your own terms, not by the whims of others or temporary distractions.

When you apply discipline to every area of life, from work to health, finances, and beyond, you free yourself from confusion and indecision, gaining the clarity to make empowered decisions. Discipline enables you to move forward with purpose, focused on what truly matters, and able to avoid the tyranny of last-minute decisions and impulsive actions.

The Challenge: Embrace the Paradox

To experience the paradox of discipline, start by committing to one small discipline for 30 days. Whether it's waking up at the same time, tracking your expenses, or completing a daily workout, make a consistent change. As you track your progress, you'll begin to see how discipline removes chaos, allowing you to make better decisions and pursue your goals with greater confidence.

At the end of the 30 days, reflect on how your life has changed:

- Did you feel more in control?
- Was your mental clarity sharper?
- Did you experience less anxiety?

The Discipline for Freedom System

Every great journey requires a map, a system to keep you on course when distractions and obstacles arise. Without a clear system, it's easy to get lost in the noise of daily life, overwhelmed by decisions, and lose sight of your long-term goals. The Discipline for Freedom System (DFS) is your framework to stay focused, measure progress, and continually make decisions that lead you toward your vision. It's a blend of Personal Navigation and Protective Discipline, guiding you through both external challenges and internal growth.

What is the Discipline for Freedom System?

The Discipline for Freedom System is a set of practices, routines, and tools that help you stay on track in all areas of your life: health, career, relationships, and personal growth. It transforms your goals into daily actions, ensuring each step aligns with your larger vision. Think of it as both a mental framework and a practical guide to living with purpose, structure, and freedom.

Much like a GPS, your DFS provides regular updates and recalculations, helping you stay on course despite life's bumps. It's not about perfection, it's about progress.

The Core Elements of the Discipline for Freedom System

Here are the 5 key components that form the core of your system:

1. Daily Routines: Building Your Foundation

- Discipline is anchored in non-negotiable daily habits. This includes routines like morning rituals (e.g., exercise, meditation) and evening practices that help you reflect and reset.

- These routines provide structure, ensuring that you start each day with purpose and end it with clarity.

2. Goal Setting & Reflection: Navigating with Intention

- Your system helps set clear, actionable goals and breaks larger objectives into manageable tasks.
- Regular reflection on progress keeps you aligned with your larger vision, allowing you to adjust when needed and ensure continuous movement forward.
- Example: If your goal is to write a book, break it into smaller tasks, such as writing a chapter a week, setting deadlines, and tracking word count daily.

3. Accountability Mechanisms: The Power of Consistency

- Accountability is essential. Incorporate methods to track habits, set regular check-ins with a mentor or accountability partner, or use apps to monitor your progress.
- Accountability ensures consistent action, making sure you follow through with plans and commitments.

4. Mental Clarity Tools: Strengthening Your Focus

- Practices like journaling, meditation, or visualization help clear mental clutter and enhance focus.
- Mental clarity is vital in maintaining discipline. These tools ensure you're aligned with your goals and can resist distractions.

5. Decisions with Confidence: Leading Your Life

- The DFS empowers you to make decisions based on your long-term vision, not fleeting emotions or external pressures.
- You'll have confidence knowing that each decision fits into your framework, reducing stress and anxiety.

Why the Discipline for Freedom System Leads to Freedom?

The paradox of discipline is simple: it doesn't restrict you; it frees you. With clear routines, structured decision-making, and intentional goals, you remove the chaos that holds you back. The more disciplined you become, the more freedom you have to pursue your goals, make confident choices, and focus on what matters most.

Incorporating this system into your life provides control over your time and energy. You won't waste mental energy deciding what to do next or feeling overwhelmed by distractions. Instead, you'll act with purpose and confidence, knowing every step brings you closer to your desired outcome.

The Challenge Create Your Discipline for Freedom System

Now, it's time to design your own Discipline for Freedom System. Here's how:

1. Reflect on your long-term goals in key areas:

- Health: How do you want to feel physically in 6 months, 1 year, 5 years?
- Career: What milestone are you working toward in your professional journey?

- Relationships: How can you improve your connections with others?

2. Break goals into actionable steps.

- Create daily routines to support these goals and establish accountability to ensure consistent progress.

💡 *Action Step:* For the next 7 days, commit to following your Discipline for Freedom System, track your progress each day and reflect on how it feels to have structure and clarity guiding your actions. At the end of the week, ask yourself:

- Did you follow your routines?
- Did you achieve your small tasks?
- How did this system impact your mental clarity and focus?

By building your Discipline for Freedom System, you create a life of intentional action, free from confusion. Your system will be your blueprint for long-term success, enabling you to move toward your goals with clarity and confidence.

Closing Principle: The Power of Discipline as Freedom

Discipline is often seen as a restriction; something that limits freedom, forces you to give up pleasures, and places demands on your time. However, the truth is that discipline is the foundation of all freedom. It's about saying "no" to distractions and "yes" to what matters. The paradox is simple: discipline creates the freedom to pursue your goals without being shackled by impulsive decisions, chaos, or uncertainty.

The more disciplined you are, the more freedom you gain. You don't have to react to life's demands because you've already created a structure that keeps you grounded. You don't need to worry about getting things done because your routine carries you through each day. Discipline becomes your tool to design your life on your terms, free from the distractions that often limit your potential.

Discipline is a daily choice, and through consistent action, it becomes the most powerful tool for achieving the freedom you seek. Embrace discipline to unlock your full potential and live the life you've always wanted.

Final Word

Discipline stands as the foundational pillar of the protective mindset. It is not a concept that can be outsourced, borrowed, or faked. It must be embodied.

In both the military and business, I've witnessed firsthand the consequences of a lack of discipline. In the military, it meant life or death. In business, it determined whether contracts were won or lost. The result is always the same: without discipline, failure is inevitable. With discipline, progress becomes unavoidable.

As we move into the next chapter, remember this: every decision, every mindset shift, and every action we discuss from here forward is built on this bedrock. Without discipline, the protective mindset will falter. With it, you'll find control amidst chaos.

Application Prompt 1: Small Habit to Build Consistency

Identify one small habit you've neglected such as consistent wake-ups, budgeting, or fitness. Turn it into a non-negotiable daily practice for the next seven days. Track your progress and reflect on how it strengthens your discipline and consistency.

Application Prompt 2: Identify and Stabilize Chaos

Identify one area in your life; work, family, or personal life where chaos frequently disrupts you. Implement one system or routine this week to stabilize it, such as organizing your tasks or prioritizing your goals. Reflect daily on how this disciplined action reduces chaos and enhances control.

Application Prompt 3: Confront Discomfort for Growth

Identify one discomfort you've been avoiding; physical, mental, or emotional. Confront it deliberately this week and commit to taking action. Reflect on how facing this discomfort builds strength and contributes to your growth.

CHAPTER
2

The Brain's Blueprint: How Habits Shape Reality

Every outcome in life whether success or failure, discipline or disorder can be traced back to the invisible power of habits. Habits are the silent architects of human behavior, often running in the background, influencing decisions, actions, and results without requiring constant conscious thought. As creatures of habit, our lives are, in many ways, an aggregate of the habits we cultivate. Success, failure, happiness, and even our sense of self-control can all be understood through the habits we build and reinforce.

Every morning, the moment a person wakes up, they begin executing habits whether it's checking their phone, making coffee, or scrolling through social media. These daily rituals become so ingrained that they no longer require much conscious thought. The brain in its effort to conserve energy, builds patterns, habits that automate behavior, making daily tasks quicker and easier. This is the brain's way of reducing mental load, enabling focus on more complex tasks.

Here's the crucial truth: the brain does not differentiate between habits that serve us and those that hinder us. The habits you form today will shape the outcomes of tomorrow. And, more importantly, discipline is the tool that empowers us to choose which habits to build, change, or remove.

How Habits Shape Reality

Habits are more than just routines; they are the invisible forces that shape our reality. Daily habits are not merely reflections of actions; they are the driving forces that determine future outcomes. Success doesn't happen by chance. It is the result of intentional, consistent habits practiced over time. The disciplined individual understands this truth: success is not a matter of luck, but the result of intentionally developed habits.

Take, for example, a professional who follows a structured routine in their daily life whether it's how they wake up, how they train, eat, or rest. Every action is part of a well-crafted system designed for peak performance. These habits do not depend on fleeting motivation or inspiration. Instead, they are automatic actions driven by discipline, fueling long-term success. A disciplined individual commit to daily practice, even when motivation fades, creating routines that become second nature, ultimately aligning them with consistent achievement.

The Discipline to Shape Your Habits

When habits shape reality, what happens when those habits no longer align with desired goals? This is where discipline plays a pivotal role. Discipline forms the foundation for both creating new habits and breaking unproductive ones. Without discipline, habits remain unconscious patterns, often shaped by external influences, impulses, or past experiences. Discipline, however, enables individuals to take control of these patterns, reshape them, and align them with long-term objectives.

A disciplined individual does not rely on fleeting motivation to take action. Instead, they design systems that carry them through challenges, especially when motivation diminishes. Discipline guarantees consistent action, allowing individuals to build lives of intention and focus, even when initial enthusiasm fades.

Why Discipline and Habits Go Hand-in-Hand

The relationship between discipline and habits is cyclical: the more discipline applied to building good habits, the easier it becomes to stay disciplined. As habits form, they require less effort to execute, reinforcing the discipline that created them. In essence, discipline lays the foundation for new habits, and habits, in turn, reinforce discipline. This creates a self-sustaining cycle of positive change.

Consider an individual who follows a morning routine that includes exercise, journaling, and planning for the day. Initially, this routine requires significant discipline to follow through. However, as the routine becomes habitual, it starts to feel automatic. Over time, less discipline is needed to complete the routine, as the habit itself drives the behavior.

This illustrates the power of discipline in action. It's not simply about forcing daily actions but about creating systems that guide decisions and actions towards long-term success.

The Habit Loop: How Habits Form

At the core of habit formation lies a powerful concept known as the habit loop, which consists of three essential components: cue, routine, and reward. Understanding how these elements interact is crucial to recognizing how habits form and more importantly, how they can be reprogrammed to better align with long-term goals.

- Cue: The habit begins with a trigger; an event, emotion, time of day, or situation that signals the brain to start the habit loop. This cue prompts the brain to go into automatic mode, initiating the process.
- Routine: The next phase in the loop is the routine, the specific behavior or action taken after the cue. This could be physical, mental, or emotional, such as a workout, checking a phone, or journaling.
- Reward: The reward is the benefit received from completing the routine. This could be the satisfaction of a task completed, the dopamine boost from social media, or the pleasure of eating comfort food. These rewards reinforce the behavior, making it more likely that the loop will repeat in the future.

The Role of the Basal Ganglia

The basal ganglia are a part of the brain responsible for habit formation. When behaviors are repeated over time, the basal ganglia automate them, creating neural shortcuts. This means that, after repetition, the behavior can occur almost automatically, without conscious thought.

The basal ganglia do not differentiate between productive or unproductive habits. Whether the habit is healthy (like daily exercise) or harmful (like smoking), the brain treats both with equal efficiency—they both become automatic.

This is where discipline comes into play. To take control over habits, it is essential to consciously manage the cues, routines, and rewards that influence daily actions. Through discipline, an individual can reprogram the brain to reinforce habits aligned with their long-term goals.

The Role of Dopamine: Why Rewards Matter

Dopamine is a neurotransmitter that plays a crucial role in habit formation. It is often referred to as the "feel-good" chemical because it is released when an individual experiences pleasure or satisfaction. However, dopamine's role extends beyond simply making someone feel good.

When a reward follows a completed routine, dopamine spikes in anticipation of the reward not just after the behavior is completed. This reinforces the habit, making it more likely to be repeated. This is why habits can form quickly around behaviors like checking a phone or indulging in unhealthy food. Dopamine reinforces the connection between the behavior and the reward.

The challenge arises when the reward is short-term gratification, such as immediate pleasure from social media or unhealthy eating. In such cases, the dopamine-driven loop can work against long-term success. Discipline is key to managing this system, as it allows the individual to replace unhealthy habits with more productive behaviors aligned with long-term goals.

By consistently applying discipline, an individual can take control of the reward system, ensuring that actions and habits reinforce the long-term Protective Discipline System rather than reinforcing immediate gratification that may derail long-term success.

Taking Control of the Habit Loop

The key to breaking bad habits and forming new, positive ones lies in discipline. Discipline has the power to reprogram the brain, enabling individuals to rewrite the habit loop in ways that better serve their long-term goals. The first step in this process is recognizing the current cues, routines, and rewards.

For instance, when attempting to break the habit of mindlessly scrolling through social media during the evening, the habit loop can be reprogrammed as follows:

- Identify the Cue: The cue could be emotional triggers, such as boredom or stress, particularly at the end of the workday.
- Create a New Routine: Instead of the habitual scrolling, a new behavior can be adopted, such as reading for 15 minutes or journaling thoughts.
- Reward the New Routine: The reward could be the sense of calm achieved from journaling or the personal growth felt from reading. These rewards reinforce the new behavior, helping to release dopamine and solidify the new routine.

By consistently applying discipline to stick with this new routine, the brain gradually adapts to expect the reward from the new behavior, making it easier to continue with the new habit. Over time, the behavior becomes automatic, and the reliance on willpower decreases, as the habit is now integrated into the routine.

Why Discipline Isn't Just About Willpower

Many mistakenly believe that willpower alone is enough to break bad habits. The challenge with willpower is that it is limited and often fluctuates. On any given day, the ability to resist temptation may vary based on factors like sleep, stress levels, or the number of decisions already made.

Discipline, on the other hand, involves creating systems that minimize the need for constant decision-making. By automating positive behaviors through new habits, willpower is no longer the primary driver. Discipline enables the design of environments and actions that make positive habits inevitable.

For instance, individuals might find it helpful to set out their workout clothes the night before, prep meals ahead of time, or set reminders for meditation. These systems remove the reliance on willpower, as they integrate the desired actions into an already established routine.

Neuroplasticity – Rewiring the Brain

The human brain is plastic, meaning it has the ability to change and adapt in response to behaviors, experiences, and environmental factors. This adaptability is known as neuroplasticity the brain's capacity to reorganize itself by forming new neural connections. Whether it's the process of learning new skills, developing better habits, or adapting to a changed mindset, repetition plays a key role in rewiring the brain, transforming new actions into automatic behaviors.

Each time a behavior is repeated, the brain strengthens the neural pathways that support it. The more frequently an action is performed, the stronger these connections become, making the behavior easier and more automatic over time. This is how habits are formed the more you engage in a specific action, the more the brain automates that action. Eventually, these behaviors become second nature.

However, neuroplasticity does not discriminate between positive and negative habits. Whether building a healthy habit, such as regular exercise, or reinforcing a detrimental behavior like procrastination, the brain adapts to whatever patterns are repeatedly enacted. This means that if negative habits are continuously repeated, they will become ingrained just as easily.

This is why discipline is essential, it allows individuals to take control of the brain's neural pathways, reshaping them to support positive, goal-oriented habits.

Neuroplasticity and Habit Formation: The Power of Repetition

When discussing habits, we are referring to repetition. The more an action or behavior is repeated, the stronger the neural pathways become. Neuroplasticity plays a pivotal role in this process. Each time a behavior is repeated whether it's exercise, eating healthy, or engaging in an unproductive habit—the brain strengthens the neural connections involved.

For instance, when someone learns a new skill for the first time like mastering a sport or a physical activity it can be challenging. Initially, the brain struggles to coordinate movements, but through continued practice, these behaviors become more automatic. Over time, these actions require less mental effort, and the brain strengthens the neural pathways that support the behavior, making it automatic.

This same process happens with daily habits, whether productive (like regular exercise) or unproductive (such as checking social media during work). The more frequently a habit is repeated, the stronger the behavior becomes, reinforcing it over time. It is not enough to understand that habits form through repetition; what is crucial is recognizing that discipline allows individuals to take control of these repetitive patterns, shaping them into positive behaviors that support long-term success.

The Power of Repetition: Neurons That Fire Together, Wire Together

One of the key principles of neuroplasticity is: "Neurons that fire together, wire together." This means that when you repeatedly engage in the same behavior or thought pattern, the neurons responsible for that action strengthen their connection, making the behavior more automatic.

For instance, when a person consistently practices a skill whether it's physical activity, learning a new concept, or addressing emotional responses, they are rewiring their brain to make those actions smoother and more automatic. The same process applies to emotional habits; if someone consistently reacts to stress with anxiety, their brain strengthens this emotional response over time, and it becomes automatic.

However, neuroplasticity is neutral. It doesn't distinguish between productive or destructive behaviors. Whether a person consistently practices positive habits like exercising or maintaining a healthy routine or engages in harmful behaviors like procrastination or unhealthy eating, the brain will reinforce them equally. The brain simply adapts to whatever behavior is repeated.

That's why discipline is so crucial. Through the application of discipline, you can intentionally reshape your habits, reprogramming your brain to support your long-term goals. Discipline is the tool that allows you to consciously direct this process, transforming your behaviors to align with the positive actions required for success. The Protective Discipline System (PDS) empowers you to break free from unproductive patterns and build habits that serve your best interests, guiding your brain's rewiring in the direction of your long-term vision.

Discipline: Reprogramming Your Brain for Success

Discipline is the key tool that enables you to harness neuroplasticity to your advantage. While neuroplasticity forms habits, it is discipline that directs this process. It involves deliberately choosing to repeat behaviors that will bring you closer to your long-term goals, rather than allowing old, automatic patterns to control your actions.

To break free from unproductive habits and cultivate new ones, you must consciously select new behaviors and commit to practicing them consistently until they become ingrained. This process requires effort, repetition, and time. Discipline allows the brain to adapt to these positive changes, ultimately making the new behavior automatic.

The Power of Small Shifts: Gradual Change and Scaling

The brain tends to resist drastic changes. When attempting major shifts, the brain perceives them as threatening and often overwhelming. The key to sustainable habit formation is gradual scaling, making small, consistent shifts rather than drastic changes. For example, instead of committing to a major overhaul, begin by setting a small, achievable goal like 5 minutes of jogging or a single push-up. Over time, as your brain adapts, you can scale the effort.

Reshaping the Blueprint: Three Strategies for Habit Mastery

Now that we understand how habits form in the brain, it's time to take control of the habit loop and start reshaping behaviors. Three core strategies can be used to change habits effectively: replacement, stacking, and gradual scaling. These strategies allow you to replace unproductive habits with positive ones, fostering lasting change.

Each strategy works in tandem with discipline the intentional practice of repeating productive behaviors consistently. Here's a breakdown of each:

Strategy 1: Replacement

Replacing a bad habit with a positive one is a powerful strategy for habit change. Rather than trying to erase a habit, replace it with a better behavior. The cue (trigger) stays the same, but the routine shifts to produce a more productive result.

For example, if you often indulge in unhealthy snacks when stressed, you could replace that behavior by drinking water or taking a short walk. The cue (stress) remains, but the routine changes, leading to a healthier outcome.

Strategy 2: Stacking

Habit stacking is a simple yet powerful strategy. This involves linking a new habit to an existing one. Since the existing habit is already ingrained in your brain, the new habit becomes associated with it.

For example, if you already have a habit of making coffee in the morning, you can stack a new habit, such as writing down three goals for the day, immediately after brewing your coffee. The established habit acts as the cue for the new behavior, making it easier to form.

Strategy 3: Gradual Scaling

Gradual scaling is an effective way to form new habits. The brain resists drastic changes, so starting small and building gradually is crucial.

For instance, if your goal is to improve fitness, don't begin by committing to an hour-long workout. Start with just 5 minutes of light exercise. Over time, as your body adapts, gradually increase the intensity and duration. Small steps lead to big results over time.

Reflection Prompt

- What habit would you like to replace?
- What action can you take today to begin this shift?
- What small change can you implement today toward your desired behavior?

Putting It All Together: Applying the Strategies

To effectively reshape habits, follow these steps:

Step 1: Identify the Habit to Change

Choose a habit you'd like to replace. Identify the cue that triggers this habit. For example, it could be an emotional response, time of day, or a particular situation.

Step 2: Choose a Replacement

Find a positive behavior to replace the negative habit. Instead of procrastination, for example, someone might replace it with a brief, productive task like organizing one's workspace or taking a few minutes to refocus. The key is to replace the routine with something that aligns with your long-term goals.

Step 3: Stack the Habit

Link the new habit to an existing routine. For example, after completing a well-established habit, like checking emails, you could add a new action, such as setting priorities for the next task.

Step 4: Scale Gradually

Begin with a small version of the new habit and increase its intensity or duration over time. Gradual changes ensure the habit becomes ingrained and sustainable.

CHAPTER 3

Discipline in Action

The Core of Discipline

Discipline is the ability to choose what matters most over what feels easiest. It is not about punishment; it is about power. True discipline is the bridge between intent and achievement, the force that turns vision into reality. Without discipline, talent and intelligence scatter. With it, even the most ordinary person can build an extraordinary life.

Discipline is not just a concept; it's a powerful, actionable force that shapes every area of life. It's not just about doing the hard thing, but about doing the right thing consistently, regardless of how easy or difficult the immediate task feels.

At its core, discipline is about control. It's the control of self, time, and choices. It's what allows you to choose what matters most when distractions demand attention. Discipline is the overseer of habits. Habits lay the foundation, but it is discipline that ensures the building is structurally sound. While habits help us automate behaviors, discipline gives us the direction and intent behind them.

The Architect of Your Future: Discipline and Direction

Think of habits as the bricks, but discipline is the architect who places them into a structure. Habits, left without discipline, can become aimless routines that don't lead to any significant progress. Discipline, however, ensures that your habits are purpose-driven, strategically designed to lead you to success.

Discipline is not about perfection; it's about consistency. Missing once is forgivable, but quitting breaks the chain. It's the difference between someone who says, "I'll try", and someone who declares, "I will."

Discipline: A Consistent Commitment

Discipline is what bridges the gap between intentions and actions. It is the consistent commitment to carrying out your plan—even when it gets uncomfortable. Discipline is about making small, deliberate decisions over time, rather than expecting instant results or relying on motivation. It's the momentum built by consistent effort, regardless of emotional state or external circumstances.

Think of your goals as a train. Each small decision you make is a piece of coal fueling the engine, pushing you toward your destination. Discipline keeps the train moving steadily, even when the track is hard to navigate or when the destination seems distant.

Practical Exercise: Cultivating Consistency

To develop discipline, start by focusing on one area of life where you currently lack consistency. Here's how you can begin:

- Choose a task or habit you've been putting off, or one that requires more consistency (e.g., daily exercise, writing, or learning).
- Set a specific goal: For instance, commit to doing 10 minutes of exercise each morning or writing for 15 minutes each day.
- Track your success daily. Each day you complete your task, check it off your list. Repetition builds momentum.

By tracking your progress, you turn discipline into a habit, and consistency becomes second nature.

Discipline Across Environments

Discipline is not confined to a single area of life. It spans across all aspects; military, business, health, relationships, and crisis management. In each of these environments, discipline is the core driver of success, enabling individuals to thrive even under pressure.

Discipline in the Military: Precision and Survival

In high-stakes environments like the military, discipline ensures that soldiers follow orders without hesitation, perform complex tasks under stress, and execute missions with precision. It enables soldiers to act swiftly and automatically in high-pressure situations, even when the stakes are life or death. Soldiers follow structured routines and systems, relying on training and discipline rather than fluctuating motivation to execute their tasks flawlessly.

Discipline in Business: Leading with Purpose

In the business world, discipline is essential for effective decision-making, time management, and goal-setting. A disciplined leader stays focused on long-term objectives and ensures resources are allocated effectively. By holding themselves accountable and setting high standards, disciplined business leaders lead by example, steering their organizations toward sustainable success, even when distractions arise.

Discipline in Health: Daily Decisions for Long-Term Success

In health, discipline is reflected in the small consistent decisions made every day in choosing nutritious foods, committing to regular exercise, or allowing time for rest. Health is not about one big decision but the repeated choices that, over time, build a foundation for long-term well-being. The disciplined individual understands that health is achieved through consistent actions, even when motivation is low.

Discipline in Relationships: Patience and Presence

In relationships, discipline manifests as consistency in showing up for others, honoring commitments, and practicing patience. It involves building trust through small, intentional acts of kindness, listening, and supporting one another. The disciplined individual remains present and dependable, strengthening relationships over time through thoughtful, consistent actions.

Discipline in Crisis: Staying Calm Under Pressure

When a crisis arises whether financial, emotional, or physical, discipline prevents panic and maintains focus. A disciplined individual, when faced with a crisis, does not react impulsively. Instead, they follow a structured system to assess the situation, make strategic decisions, and stay calm under pressure. This ability to remain composed is cultivated through years of disciplined practice in decision-making and emotional regulation.

Tools of Discipline

Discipline is a muscle that requires continuous strengthening and practice. Just like physical strength is built over time, mental discipline grows through consistent use of specific tools. These tools help structure your day, keep you on track, and ensure that your discipline remains focused and effective.

Rather than relying solely on willpower which can fade under stress, discipline thrives when it is supported by structured systems and intentional practices. Below are powerful tools you can use to cultivate discipline in your daily life.

Time-Blocking: Guard Your Time

Time is one of the most valuable resources we have, and how we use it directly impacts our productivity and well-being. Time-blocking is a tool that helps you take control of your day by allocating specific blocks of time for specific tasks.

How It Works:

- Plan Your Day: At the beginning of each day (or the night before), schedule out your time. Assign specific hours for work, exercise, meals, relaxation, and any other important tasks.
- No Multitasking: When you time-block, dedicate your full attention to one task at a time. This minimizes distractions and enhances focus.
- Protect Your Time: Once you've assigned a time block, stick to it. Guard this time from distractions, treating it as non-negotiable.

By using time-blocking, you take the guesswork out of your day. Discipline becomes easier when it is backed by a plan, and time-blocking ensures you use your time intentionally, with purpose.

Prioritization: Focus on What Matters Most

It's easy to get caught up in the day-to-day tasks, but discipline requires focus on what truly matters. Prioritization helps you direct your energy to the most important tasks those that align with your long-term goals.

How It Works:

- Identify the Most Important Task: Each day, identify the one task that will move you closest to your goals. This is your priority for the day.
- Finish It First: Before moving on to other tasks, complete this priority task to ensure you're making progress toward your long-term objectives.

- Use the "Two-Minute Rule": If a task can be completed in two minutes or less, do it immediately. This keeps your to-do list manageable and prevents small tasks from piling up.

Prioritization ensures you focus on what matters most, eliminating the feeling of being busy but not productive. It keeps your attention on tasks that lead to success.

The Power of No: Protect Your Focus

One of the most powerful tools for building discipline is the ability to say no. Every time you say yes to something, you are, in essence, saying no to something else. Saying yes to distractions or commitments that don't align with your priorities scatters your focus and erodes discipline.

How It Works:

- Be Selective with Commitments: Before saying yes to something, ask yourself, "Does this align with my goals?" If the answer is no, it's an opportunity to say no.
- Set Boundaries: Protect your time and energy by setting clear boundaries. For example, you may need to say no to last-minute meetings or activities that don't contribute to your priorities.
- Practice Saying No: Start with small requests, such as saying no to a social invitation when you need to focus on work. The more you practice saying no, the easier it becomes.

By saying no to unnecessary things, you free up time and energy to focus on what truly matters. Saying no is a tool that helps you stay consistent and disciplined.

Endurance Training: Push Beyond Comfort

Discipline requires the ability to push through discomfort. One of the most effective ways to build mental toughness is through endurance training—doing something that challenges you physically or mentally, even when you don't feel like it.

How It Works:

- Increase the Challenge Gradually: Start with small challenges that push you outside your comfort zone. For example, if you're used to exercising for 10 minutes, challenge yourself to do 12 minutes.
- Consistency Over Intensity: The goal of endurance training is to stay consistent. Instead of overwhelming yourself with a huge challenge, aim for small, consistent efforts.
- Push Through the Resistance: When your mind tells you to stop, push through for one more minute, one more set, or one more task. This builds mental resilience.

Endurance training teaches that discipline isn't about being comfortable it's about pushing through discomfort and growing stronger each day.

Trigger Elimination: Remove Temptations

Your environment plays a huge role in shaping your habits. If your environment is filled with temptations, maintaining discipline becomes difficult. Trigger elimination helps you remove distractions and create a focused environment that supports your goals.

How It Works:

- Identify Distractions: Take note of the triggers in your environment that encourage bad habits. This could include your phone, snacks on the kitchen counter, or a cluttered workspace.
- Remove Temptations: Whenever possible, eliminate distractions from your environment. For instance, leave your phone in another room while working, or store unhealthy snacks out of sight.
- Create Positive Triggers: Replace negative triggers with positive ones. For example, place your gym clothes next to your bed to remind you to work out in the morning.

Eliminating temptations from your environment reduces the effort required to stay disciplined. It's much easier to be disciplined when your surroundings align with your goals.

Accountability Systems: Reinforce Discipline with Support

Accountability is a tool that amplifies discipline. By involving others in your progress, you increase your chances of success. Accountability partners or systems reinforce your commitment and provide the support you need to stay consistent.

How It Works:

- **Find an Accountability Partner**: Choose someone who shares your goals or has a similar commitment. Share your intentions with them and ask them to check in regularly on your progress.

- **Use Digital Tools**: Apps like Habitica, StickK, or even a simple calendar can serve as accountability systems to track progress and stay on course.
- **Weekly Check-Ins**: Set up a weekly check-in with your accountability partner to evaluate progress, celebrate wins, and adjust goals if needed.

Accountability makes discipline social, it reinforces your commitments and provides external pressure that helps you stay consistent.

Discipline Drills

Discipline is a practice that must be cultivated and maintained through consistent action. The following drills are designed to challenge you and push your limits, helping to build the muscle of discipline. These exercises force you to act in alignment with your goals, even when the process feels uncomfortable. The key to mastering discipline lies in consistently choosing what is right, even when it's difficult.

The 5 AM Test: Own Your Morning

Mastering your morning sets the tone for the rest of your day. The 5 AM Test is a simple yet powerful drill that challenges you to wake up one hour earlier than usual and use that time intentionally—whether for exercise, planning, journaling, or other productive activities.

How It Works:

- Set your alarm for 5 AM (or one hour earlier than usual).
- Use the extra hour for productive activities that align with your long-term goals, such as exercising, reading, or goal-setting.

- Commit to this drill for seven consecutive days.
- Track your progress and note the impact on your energy, focus, and productivity.

This challenge not only adds time to your day but also strengthens your discipline by prioritizing your goals over comfort.

The Cold Shower Method: Embrace Discomfort

Discomfort is often seen as a barrier, but it is also a powerful tool for building discipline. The Cold Shower Method is designed to help you develop the ability to endure discomfort, which is essential for strengthening mental resilience.

How It Works:

- Turn the shower to cold and step in for two minutes.
- Focus on staying present and breathing deeply.
- Repeat this drill for seven consecutive days.
- After each session, track how you feel whether you experience a sense of energy or accomplishment.

This method helps you build mental toughness by pushing past discomfort, showing that discipline involves enduring, not avoiding, discomfort.

The Digital Fast: Disconnect to Reconnect

In today's world of constant connectivity, distractions can diminish focus and erode discipline. The Digital Fast drill requires you to disconnect from non-essential digital distractions for 24 hours.

How It Works:

- Turn off all social media accounts and unnecessary digital devices for a full 24 hours.
- Use this time to engage in real-world activities such as reading, working on a project, or having uninterrupted conversations.
- At the end of the fast, reflect on the experience: Did you feel more focused and present? How much time was consumed by distractions?

This drill helps you take control of your digital habits, reinforcing discipline in your environment.

The Accountability Partner: External Pressure for Internal Discipline

An Accountability Partner helps reinforce your commitment and holds you responsible for your progress, which strengthens discipline.

How It Works:

- Choose a goal that is meaningful and measurable.
- Share this goal with a trusted accountability partner (a friend, mentor, or colleague).
- Set up weekly check-ins where your partner checks on your progress.
- Stay consistent, knowing that you will report your progress.

Accountability introduces an external layer of responsibility that encourages consistent action and reinforces your commitment.

The Silent Meal: Mindful Eating

The Silent Meal drill helps you build discipline in the area of eating by promoting mindfulness and self-control.

How It Works:

- Eat a meal in complete silence; no distractions like TV, phones, or conversations.
- Focus on each bite, its taste, texture, and the experience of eating.
- Eat slowly, stop when you are satisfied not when you're full.
- Repeat this for every meal for a week.

This drill builds discipline around mindful choices and reminds you that small, intentional decisions matter every day.

The Extra Mile: Training Endurance in Small Ways

The Extra Mile drill encourages you to push through resistance, building endurance in small, manageable steps.

How It Works:

- Choose a task (workout, project, or personal goal).
- When you feel like quitting, push yourself to go one step further whether it's doing one more set, writing one more page, or spending five more minutes on your goal.
- Gradually, pushing past resistance becomes a habit.

This drill strengthens mental toughness and reinforces the idea that discipline is about continuing when it feels difficult.

Discipline in Leadership

Discipline is the cornerstone of effective leadership. A disciplined leader not only sets the standard but creates a culture of consistency and focus that drives the success of the team. Leadership discipline impacts everything from decision-making to how teams manage their time and priorities.

Leading by Example: The Power of Modeling Discipline

Leaders who model discipline create a culture of accountability and respect. Consistent actions speak louder than words. Leaders who show up on time, follow through with commitments, and stay focused on long-term goals set the tone for their team.

How to Lead with Discipline:

- Model Consistency: Commit to showing up on time and doing what you say you will. Your actions will define the team's behavior.
- Follow Through: Execute your commitments, which reinforces your credibility.
- Set Clear Expectations: Communicate what you expect, but also hold yourself to those same standards.
- Create Accountability: Hold your team accountable while also taking responsibility for your own actions.

Discipline in Decision-Making

A disciplined leader is confident and clear in their decision-making, even under pressure. Indecision and lack of direction are often rooted in inconsistent focus.

How to Make Decisive Choices:

- Avoid analysis paralysis.
- Stick to your values and principles.
- Make quick, confident decisions even when facing uncertainty.

Practical Exercise: The 5-Minute Rule for Decision-Making

- When faced with a decision, give yourself 5 minutes to make it. Trust your system of values and goals. Resist the urge to overthink; progress is more important than perfection.

Building a Disciplined Team

Leaders set the stage for how the team will operate. Discipline in leadership is contagious. When you model disciplined behavior, your team will likely adopt the same approach.

How to Instill Discipline in Your Team:

- Establish Clear Standards: Set high expectations for performance, focusing on consistency, effort, and accountability.
- Foster Ownership: Give your team ownership of their work, encouraging self-discipline.
- Provide Support and Resources: Ensure the team has the right tools and resources to succeed.

Discipline Through Delegation

Effective delegation is key to leadership discipline. It requires trust and the ability to let go, allowing your team members to develop their own self-discipline.

How to Delegate with Discipline:

- Set Clear Expectations: Communicate the outcome and timeline.
- Trust and Let Go: Allow your team the space to complete the task while offering support as needed.
- Follow Up with Accountability: Ensure regular check-ins to track progress.

Building Discipline Through Systems

Discipline is not just about willpower; it's about creating systems that ensure long-term success. Systems remove the need for constant decision-making, making disciplined actions automatic. They bring structure to your environment, your routines, and your processes. Without systems, discipline becomes a constant battle against distractions and temptations, which can overwhelm you. However, with the right systems in place, discipline becomes an integral part of your daily life.

The Power of Systems: Why Willpower Alone Doesn't Work

While willpower is essential for making decisions in the moment, it's limited and can fatigue over time. You can't rely solely on willpower to carry you through the day or the task at hand. This is where systems come in. They provide the structure that makes it easier to stay disciplined, even when motivation wanes.

Think of willpower as the fuel in a car: it powers the car for a while, but it eventually runs out. Systems are the engine that keeps the car moving consistently, even when the fuel is low.

The Importance of Morning Rituals

One of the most powerful systems you can build is a morning ritual. How you start your day sets the tone for everything that follows. A disciplined morning routine ensures that you begin your day with intentionality, focusing on actions that align with your goals.

How It Works:

- Wake up early: Give yourself at least 30-60 minutes before starting your work or other obligations.
- Engage in mindful activities: Use this time for exercise, meditation, journaling, or reading activities that align with your personal and professional goals.
- Plan your day: Set your intentions for the day. Identify the one thing that will move you closest to your goals. What are your priorities?

By establishing a disciplined morning routine, you set a purposeful tone for the day ahead. It primes you to approach your tasks with the same level of focus, discipline, and consistency.

The Role of Review Cycles: Tracking Progress

Discipline requires accountability, and review cycles provide the feedback necessary to stay on track. Without a way to measure your progress, it's easy to become complacent or lose sight of your goals.

How It Works:

- Set a weekly review: At the end of each week, take time to assess your progress. What went well? What didn't?
- Measure your performance: Track your goals and habits. Did you complete your daily workouts? Did you stick to your time-blocking schedule?
- Adjust your approach: Use this feedback to refine your systems for the next week. If something isn't working, change it. If something is working, double down on it.

Weekly reviews help you stay accountable and ensure that your systems are functioning effectively. They also allow you to course-correct before small problems become bigger obstacles.

Environment Design: Creating the Right Setting for Discipline

Your environment plays a huge role in shaping your discipline. If your environment is filled with distractions, it becomes much harder to stay focused. But when you design your environment to support your goals, you make discipline easier and more automatic.

How It Works:

- Eliminate temptations: If you want to avoid unhealthy snacks, don't keep them in your house. If you're trying to cut down on screen time, keep your phone out of reach during work hours.

- Design for success: Set up your workspace for maximum productivity. Keep tools, resources, and reminders aligned with your goals.
- Create visual triggers: Use post-it notes, reminders, or visual cues to help reinforce your goals. For example, place a motivational quote or your top priorities on your desk.

By designing your environment to align with your goals, you reduce the friction between intention and action.

Non-Negotiables: Protect What Matters Most

One of the most powerful ways to ensure discipline is to identify non-negotiables; the areas of your life that cannot be compromised, no matter how busy or stressful your day becomes.

How It Works:

- Identify your non-negotiables: What is most important to you? These could be family dinners, gym sessions, or financial reviews. Choose areas that align with your long-term goals and well-being.
- Protect these areas fiercely: Treat your non-negotiables as sacred. Set boundaries around these activities and guard your time.
- Make them non-negotiable: Commit to these actions every day, no exceptions. If something else comes up, find a way to adjust but never compromise on these core activities.

Non-negotiables provide the structure to maintain discipline, even when life gets busy or chaotic. When you protect what matters most, you ensure that discipline remains the foundation of your life.

Common Enemies of Discipline

Discipline is a continuous process, and the path to success is often filled with obstacles and temptations that can derail even the most focused efforts. These "enemies" are often subtle forces that pull us away from our goals. Identifying and overcoming these distractions is key to strengthening your discipline and achieving long-term success. In this section, we'll explain common enemies of discipline; comfort, distraction, excuses, and inconsistency also outline practical strategies to counteract them.

Comfort: The Silent Killer of Discipline

Comfort can be the most deceptive enemy of discipline. It whispers, "You've worked hard enough today," or "It's okay to take it easy just this once." While comfort may seem inviting, it leads to stagnation. Discipline thrives in discomfort, pushing through challenges, overcoming resistance, and doing what needs to be done, even when it's difficult.

How to Overcome Comfort:

- Set High Standards: Ask yourself, "Is this the best I can do?" The more rigorous your standards, the less room comfort has to take over.

- Embrace Discomfort: Gradually incorporate challenges into your routine. The discomfort will soon feel normal, and your discipline will become stronger.
- Push Past Resistance: When comfort pulls you to procrastinate, do the opposite. Take action immediately. Go for a run or tackle a task you've been avoiding. The more you push back, the easier it becomes to stay disciplined.

Distraction: The Enemy of Focus

In a world overflowing with distractions from social media notifications to constant digital noise maintaining focus is a major challenge. Distraction scatters your energy and prevents you from committing to your goals. When distractions take control, they dilute your clarity and focus, essential elements for achieving sustained success.

How to Overcome Distraction:

- Remove External Distractions: Put your phone on silent, close unnecessary browser tabs, and clear your workspace of clutter. A focused environment encourages disciplined behavior.
- Use Time-Blocking: Set designated times for work and leisure. Stick to the schedule and minimize distractions during focused work periods.
- Practice Deep Focus: Work in focused bursts using techniques like the Pomodoro method (25 minutes of focused work followed by a 5-minute break)—to train your mind to resist distractions.

Excuses: The Mind's Justification for Inaction

Excuses are a powerful enemy that rationalizes avoidance, discomfort, and fear of failure. These thoughts; "I don't have time," "It's too hard," or "I'm not ready" are convincing, but they only keep you stuck. Overcoming excuses requires awareness and taking immediate action, even when discomfort or fear creeps in.

How to Overcome Excuses:

- Recognize the Excuse: When you hear yourself making excuses, pause and reflect: Is this really true? Or am I just avoiding discomfort?
- Challenge the Excuse: Ask yourself, "What if I did it anyway?" Often, the fear of failure is more overwhelming than the actual task.
- Take Immediate Action: Combat excuses with action. For instance, if you're avoiding exercise, simply put on your workout clothes and do five minutes of activity. Starting is often the hardest part.

Inconsistency: The Path to Mediocrity

Inconsistency is a quiet killer of discipline. Starting strong is easy, but maintaining that effort is what separates high achievers from those who falter. When inconsistent, your progress will fluctuate, making it impossible to build the momentum needed for success. Discipline requires steadiness; the ability to show up every day, regardless of your emotional state or external circumstances.

How to Overcome Inconsistency:

- Start Small and Build Gradually: Focus on one habit at a time. Build consistency in that area before adding more changes.
- Use Tracking Systems: Keep track of your habits and progress. The visual reinforcement of your progress will keep you motivated to stay consistent.
- Make It Non-Negotiable: Turn your habits into non-negotiables. Treat them like an appointment that can't be missed. For instance, once you start your day with a workout, treat it as a commitment you cannot skip.

The Link Between Discipline and Trust

Discipline and trust are deeply interconnected in leadership. Trust is not built on words or promises alone; it is earned through consistent action over time. Discipline forms the foundation upon which trust is built. By consistently following through on commitments, meeting deadlines, and staying focused on your goals, you establish credibility and reliability as a leader.

In leadership, trust is one of the most valuable assets you can have. It is the currency that enables you to lead with authority, make confident decisions, and inspire others to follow. However, trust doesn't come overnight, it is earned through disciplined actions that demonstrate your commitment to your team, your values, and your goals.

Trust is Built Through Consistency

Trust is not a single event; it is a process that evolves over time. It is about showing up consistently and doing what you say you will do. The more reliable you are, the more your team or colleagues will trust you.

How Discipline Builds Trust:

- Reliability: Consistent discipline demonstrates reliability. Leaders who follow through on their commitments earn the trust of their team.
- Accountability: Discipline reinforces personal accountability. A disciplined leader holds themselves to high standards, encouraging others to do the same.
- Transparency: Discipline involves transparency. When your actions align with your values and goals, you build trust by showing others where you stand.

Trust and Leadership: The Foundation of Strong Teams

Discipline creates an environment where trust can thrive. A leader who is consistent in their actions, words, and decisions fosters trust within their team. Discipline in leadership is not about controlling others; it's about being a role model who inspires discipline through their own actions.

When your team sees that you are disciplined, they feel more confident in the direction of the organization. They trust your vision, your commitment, and your decisions because you have demonstrated the ability to act consistently and with purpose.

How to Build Trust Through Discipline as a Leader:

- Be Consistent: Show up every day, make decisions that align with your values, and be reliable. Trust is built when others know they can rely on you.
- Lead by Example: Model the behaviors you expect from your team. Your discipline will encourage others to follow suit.
- Follow Through on Commitments: Never promise what you can't deliver. Consistent follow-through builds trust.

Case Studies of Discipline in Leadership

Discipline is the cornerstone of effective leadership. The most successful leaders don't simply lead—they lead with discipline. Their ability to maintain focus, consistency, and resolve, even in the face of challenges, sets them apart. Below are several real-world examples of leaders whose discipline has significantly impacted their success. These case studies demonstrate how discipline is not just a personal trait, but a leadership strategy that can shape the trajectory of a team or organization.

Case Study 1: The Entrepreneur's Grind

One of the most challenging aspects of entrepreneurship is the uncertainty that comes with it. Leaders in startup environments often face limited resources, long hours, and the threat of failure. Yet, those who succeed are often the ones who discipline themselves to stick to a routine, focus on long-term goals, and persevere through adversity.

The Story:

A leader in a startup faced a critical moment with limited funding remaining. Despite mounting pressure, she implemented a disciplined schedule: five hours of daily product development, three hours for customer outreach, and two hours for investor relations. She adhered to this schedule, even when results weren't immediately visible.

Key Takeaway:

Discipline is about sticking to the plan even when results aren't immediate. Consistency and focused effort create momentum, which eventually leads to breakthroughs.

Case Study 2: The Athlete's Edge

In sports, discipline is not just about physical training it's about mental toughness and consistency. The most successful athletes show up every day, regardless of external circumstances, ensuring that their success is a result of disciplined, daily routines.

The Story:

An Olympic athlete, despite extreme weather conditions, adhered to her training schedule every day. Her competitors often skipped practice, justifying it with the need for rest. While others rested, this athlete pushed through the discomfort, training rigorously to improve her performance. When race day arrived, her discipline in training gave her a competitive edge.

Key Takeaway:

Discipline in leadership isn't just about hard work; it's about showing up every day, even when it's difficult. Consistency gives leaders a competitive advantage over others who may be more talented but less disciplined.

Case Study 3: The Security Professional

In high-stakes environments, the most disciplined professionals stay alert and prepared for the unexpected. Their ability to maintain focus for extended periods, even without incident, is critical to their success.

The Story:

A security professional stationed at a high-risk facility faced long shifts, often lasting up to 12 hours, with no immediate threats. The temptation to relax was constant, but the officer remained vigilant. When an emergency arose, her disciplined focus allowed her to act swiftly, preventing a potential crisis.

Key Takeaway:

Discipline in leadership means focus and preparedness. It's about staying alert and ready, even when there is no immediate danger. A disciplined leader anticipates challenges and responds with consistency.

Closing Thoughts: Discipline as Destiny

Discipline is more than a tool, it is the foundation upon which success is built. In every area of life, from personal growth to leadership, discipline is the force that propels you forward. It bridges the gap between intentions and results, transforming goals into reality. Discipline doesn't require grand gestures; it's about small, consistent actions that compound over time to create extraordinary outcomes.

The most successful leaders, athletes, entrepreneurs, and achievers understand that discipline shapes their destiny. They don't wait for inspiration or external circumstances to align, they take deliberate, disciplined action, day in and day out. By building systems that support their goals, they turn their vision into a structured plan and create habits that align with their future success.

Action Step: Commit to One Goal

Choose one specific goal you've been procrastinating on and apply consistent discipline to it every day for the next 30 days. Track your progress and reflect on how discipline impacts your ability to move forward, even when results aren't immediate.

Reflection Prompts

Reflection process allows you to identify what is working, what isn't, and how you can make adjustments to stay on track with your goals.

1. Where in your life are you most disciplined today?

Think about areas in your life where discipline is already a strength. It could be in your work, fitness, finances, or even your daily routines.

Identifying where you're already disciplined will give you confidence that you are capable of improving other areas of your life.

Action Step: Write down the areas where you excel at discipline. Celebrate those wins and use them as proof that you can apply the same approach to other areas by creating structured systems.

2. Where do you lack discipline, and what is the cost of that weakness?

Everyone has areas where they struggle with discipline. It could be procrastination, unhealthy habits, or inconsistent work patterns. Recognizing where you lack discipline is the first step toward improvement. But also reflect on the cost—what does this lack of discipline cost you in terms of time, opportunities, or personal growth?

Action Step: Write down the areas where you lack discipline. Be honest about the cost it has on your life, and use this awareness to fuel your motivation to improve by designing a system to address it.

3. What one area, if disciplined, would most transform your future?

Identify the one area that, if you applied more discipline, would have the biggest impact on your future. It could be learning a new skill, starting a project, or improving your health. This question helps you prioritize and focus on the area that will create the most significant change.

Action Step: Choose one specific goal that will transform your life. Create a simple, actionable plan with clear systems to implement discipline in this area over the next week.

4. How do you respond when discipline is challenged by crisis?

Discipline is often tested in times of stress or crisis. When things don't go as planned or when life throws a curveball, how do you respond? Do you break your routines, or do you maintain them despite the challenges? Reflect on how well you've maintained discipline during tough times.

Action Step: Write down a recent crisis or stressful event and reflect on how your discipline held up. What systems can you implement next time to ensure you stay disciplined, even in chaos?

5. What habit, if mastered, would most transform your life in the next six months?

Think about one habit that, if mastered, could bring about significant positive change in your life. This could be something small but impactful, like exercising regularly, tracking your finances, or reading daily. Habits compound over time, so mastering one habit can lead to massive progress.

Action Step: Choose that one habit, break it down into small steps, and commit to practicing it every day for the next month. Track your progress and build momentum through consistent actions.

6. How can you reduce friction today to make the right choice automatic?

Often, we make poor decisions because of friction—things that make it harder to act on our intentions. Friction could be a lack of preparation, distractions, or temptations in your environment. By reducing friction, you can make disciplined actions easier and more automatic.

Action Step: Identify one area of your life where friction exists (e.g., eating unhealthy foods, procrastinating on tasks). Find a small change you can make today to reduce that friction and make the right choice easier. For example, if you're trying to eat healthier, remove junk food from your house or use meal prep systems to make healthy eating easier.

4

Mastering Emotional Independence: Becoming the Anchor in Any Storm.

The Myth of External Peace

Many are conditioned from an early age to depend on external factors for their sense of stability. People seek validation and peace from outside forces whether it's grades, approval from others, or social media likes. Over time, it becomes easy to believe that feelings depend on circumstances outside of oneself.

The truth, however, is more empowering: your internal state is the only thing you can truly control. Your thoughts, emotions, and reactions are within your complete control. Mastering your inner world allows you to shape your environment, not the other way around. Failing to take responsibility for your internal state means external circumstances will inevitably dictate your emotional state, leaving you at the mercy of life's unpredictability and others' opinions.

The Illusion of External Peace

Many believe that peace can be found through external circumstances. The assumption is that once the "right job," the "perfect partner," or the "ideal bank balance" is obtained, peace will follow. External success is mistakenly equated with inner peace, creating the belief that if everything outside is aligned, happiness and fulfillment will come.

However, external peace is fragile. It is based on factors beyond one's control. A career shift, a change in relationships, or an unexpected bill can undermine the sense of peace that was once thought to be secure. True peace cannot be attained from the outside; it must be cultivated from within. Relying on external peace is like building on shifting sands—change can tear down everything built on that unstable foundation.

Internal Peace: The True Anchor

Emotional independence means not relying on external factors for peace. Like a tree with deep roots, you remain steady, even in the face of storms. Internal peace is a skill that can be developed by training the mind and emotions to remain steady, regardless of what happens around you.

Mastering emotional independence means recognizing that peace does not depend on external circumstances; it is entirely within one's control. By focusing on what can be controlled—thoughts, emotions, and responses you reclaim your power and begin to live with inner stability, regardless of external conditions.

The core principle of emotional independence is straightforward yet powerful: you cannot control the external world, but you can control your internal world. Emotional independence is the ability to manage your emotions, responses, and perceptions, regardless of what's happening around you.

External circumstances will always change. People's opinions shift, situations evolve, and life presents unexpected challenges. If your peace depends on these external factors, you'll constantly be at the mercy of outside influences. Many people fall into the trap of believing that to be happy, successful, or peaceful, their external world must align perfectly. This belief leaves them vulnerable and reactive.

True emotional independence starts with understanding that while you cannot control external events, you can control your response to them. Your emotional state is your responsibility. Once you accept this responsibility, you empower yourself to shape your reality, no matter what external challenges arise.

The Emotional Independence Paradigm

Emotional independence is not about avoiding or suppressing emotions; it's about taking full responsibility for how you process them. It's about making conscious choices in how you respond, rather than reacting impulsively or letting emotions dictate your decisions. The key principle here is separating your emotions from your decisions.

- **Processing Emotions Without Allowing Them to Control You:** Emotions are natural and inevitable, but they should not control your actions. For instance, when you feel anger, acknowledge it, but do not let it drive your decisions. Emotional independence is about pausing and choosing a response that aligns with your values.

- **Taking Responsibility for Your Reactions:** Even when others act inappropriately or circumstances are challenging, your reactions remain your responsibility. You cannot control how others behave, but you always have control over how you choose to respond. This mindset shift is essential for mastering emotional independence.

- **Building Self-Worth That Is Unshakable:** The foundation of emotional independence is a strong sense of self-worth. When your self-worth comes from within, external validation or rejection cannot sway your emotional state. You own your value, and no one else can determine it.

- **Living by Principles, Not by Moods:** Principles act as your internal compass; your values, beliefs, and guidelines for life. Emotional independence means making decisions based on these principles, not on how you feel in the moment. While moods are fleeting, principles provide a stable foundation for consistent action.

The Discipline of Emotional Independence

Mastering emotional independence is a lifelong commitment, it requires practice and dedication. It's not a quick fix, but the reward is immense: the freedom to respond to life on your own terms, without being driven by emotions or external circumstances. The more you practice emotional independence, the easier it becomes to stay grounded, even during turbulent times.

This discipline involves developing habits, strategies, and mindsets that allow you to process emotions without being controlled by them. It also requires self-awareness—recognizing when emotions are influencing your decisions and stepping back to gain clarity before you act.

The Emotional Anchor Framework

Mastering emotional independence requires a structured framework that allows you to take control of your emotional responses, especially in high-stress situations. The Emotional Anchor Framework helps you process emotions effectively and respond with intention, rather than reacting impulsively. This isn't about suppressing emotions; it's about processing them and regaining control before they influence your actions.

1. Awareness Before Action

The first step in mastering emotional independence is to become aware of your emotions as soon as they arise. The moment you feel an emotional shift whether it's anger, frustration, or anxiety it's crucial to name the emotion. Naming it creates an immediate disarming effect. By identifying the emotion, you take the first step in separating yourself from it, rather than being at the mercy of your unconscious reactions.

Why This Works:

By acknowledging and naming the emotion, you prevent it from controlling you. This awareness allows you to decide how to respond, rather than simply reacting. Emotional awareness empowers you to make conscious choices about how to handle situations.

Example:

If you feel anger when a situation doesn't go as planned, pause and name the emotion: "I'm feeling frustrated right now." This simple act of naming the emotion helps you disarm its intensity and create space for a more measured response.

2. Pause and Breathe

Once you recognize your emotional state, the next step is to pause and breathe. Taking a brief moment like 5 to 10 seconds to breathe deeply interrupts the brain's natural fight-or-flight response, which can escalate emotions like anger or anxiety. By pausing, you allow your body to regain calm and your mind to process the situation before you react.

Why This Works:

Controlled breathing reduces stress hormones like cortisol and helps restore emotional balance. This momentary pause enables you to respond thoughtfully instead of impulsively reacting.

Example:

Before replying to a message that frustrates you, take a deep breath. Count to five as you inhale, then count to five as you exhale. This practice helps regulate your emotional state, enabling a calm, thoughtful response.

3. Reframe the Event

Reframing is one of the most powerful tools for emotional independence. It involves changing your perspective on a situation. By shifting the way you interpret an event, you change the emotional response it triggers. Instead of reacting with frustration or fear, ask yourself: "What's another way to see this?"

Why This Works:

The mind can only hold one dominant interpretation of an event at a time. Reframing allows you to change that interpretation and choose a more empowering emotional response.

Example:

If you receive negative feedback at work, rather than taking it personally, reframe it as an opportunity to improve. Think, "This feedback can help me strengthen my work." This shift turns frustration into motivation.

4. Return to Your Baseline

Your baseline is the calm, centered emotional state you aim to return to when you're thrown off balance. Grounding habits like meditation, journaling, prayer, or physical exercise help reset your emotional state so you don't carry negative emotions into the next challenge.

Why This Works:

Grounding practices build emotional resilience. Having consistent rituals helps you reset and refocus, ensuring that external stressors don't derail your progress. These habits teach your mind and body to return to calm, even during adversity.

Example:

After a stressful situation, take a walk or write down your thoughts in a journal. These grounding actions help you reset so that you don't carry negative energy into your next interaction.

5. Lead with Calm

Leading with calm means acting decisively and confidently, even amid emotional turbulence. By practicing awareness, pausing, reframing, and grounding, you can respond from a place of centeredness, making clear, controlled decisions.

Why This Works:

Leading with calm is a powerful tool for influencing the emotions of others. When you remain calm, you set the emotional tone for those around you. This is particularly important in leadership or crisis situations, where your composure can steer the emotional climate.

Example:

In a tense meeting, your calm demeanor can help others regain composure. When you respond with clarity and confidence, others will be more likely to follow your lead.

Training Emotional Independence

Mastering emotional independence is like strength training repetition, consistency, and gradual progress. Just as physical fitness takes time and effort, emotional independence is cultivated through consistent, small actions.

Training emotional independence is not just about reacting to emotions as they arise; it's about proactively building habits and mindsets that help you stay centered in any situation. Over time, this foundation will support you through life's challenges.

1. Start with Small, Everyday Irritations

Emotional independence begins with the small, everyday irritations i.e the moments that often trigger emotional reactions. Whether it's a delay at work, a disagreement with a colleague, or an unexpected change in plans, these situations offer the perfect opportunity to practice emotional control.

Why This Works:

Building emotional muscle starts with the small moments. Training yourself to respond thoughtfully to minor frustrations equips you to handle larger, more stressful situations over time. Consistency is key.

Example:

In a situation like traffic congestion or a delayed appointment, pause and shift your focus. Instead of letting frustration take over, redirect your energy to something productive like focusing on your breathing, listening to a podcast, or preparing mentally for the task ahead.

2. Build Emotional Resilience in Low-Stakes Situations

After practicing emotional control in smaller situations, it's time to build resilience in slightly more challenging contexts. This might include handling stress at work, dealing with minor conflicts, or managing disappointment when things don't go as planned.

Why This Works:

By increasing the emotional challenge in manageable steps, you strengthen your ability to maintain control even when emotions are running high. These situations provide an opportunity to practice your emotional anchor framework.

Example:

In the case of a deadline approaching at work or a minor conflict with a colleague, use your emotional independence strategies. Pause, breathe, and reframe the situation. This allows you to take control of your response, reducing the likelihood of reacting impulsively.

3. Anticipate and Prepare for Emotional Triggers

As you progress in practicing emotional independence, you'll begin to notice specific triggers; people, situations, or environments that consistently provoke strong emotional reactions. The key to mastering emotional independence is to prepare for these triggers before they catch you off guard.

Why This Works:

Proactively identifying triggers gives you the ability to respond intentionally. This self-awareness is crucial for building long-lasting emotional independence.

Example:

If public speaking triggers anxiety, reframe the event by focusing on the opportunity it provides to share valuable information. Preparation allows you to control your emotional response before the event.

4. Build Emotional Strength through Daily Practices

The best way to sustain emotional independence is to integrate grounding practices into your daily routine. By doing so, you develop an emotional foundation that remains solid, regardless of external circumstances. These practices should become non-negotiable parts of your routine.

Why This Works:

Daily grounding practices reinforce emotional resilience. Over time, they become habits that automatically bring you back to a calm, centered state, no matter the stressors you face.

Example:

Incorporating activities like meditation in the morning, journaling in the evening, or taking a walk after work can reset your emotional state, preparing you to face challenges with a clear mind.

Common Traps of Emotional Dependence

Even as you work to master emotional independence, there are subtle traps that can derail your progress. These traps often hide in plain sight, influencing your emotional responses and keeping you reactive instead of proactive. Recognizing these traps is essential for anyone striving to build lasting emotional independence. By identifying them, you can avoid falling into patterns that undermine your emotional control and make better choices when emotions arise.

1. Seeking Validation from Others

One of the most common traps of emotional dependence is seeking validation from others. In today's world, it's easy to look for approval whether through social media likes, praise from colleagues, or acknowledgment from friends. While external validation can feel good in the moment, relying on it too heavily ties your emotional well-being to something you can't control.

Why This Is a Trap:

When you let other opinions determine your emotional state, you give away your power. This leaves you vulnerable to rejection, criticism, or neglect, which can shake your emotional stability. True emotional independence begins with internal validation—trusting your own decisions and affirming your worth from within.

How to Avoid It:

Recognize when you're seeking approval. Pause and ask yourself: Do I really need this validation? Reinforce your self-worth by affirming your values, goals, and decisions internally. Understand that the only validation that truly matters comes from you.

2. Holding Grudges

Holding grudges is another common trap of emotional dependence. When someone wrongs you, it's natural to feel anger or resentment. However, holding onto these emotions can cloud your judgment and prevent you from moving forward with clarity and peace.

Why This Is a Trap:

A grudge is like carrying a heavy emotional weight. It drains your energy and distracts you from what matters. You give power to past events, letting them control your current emotional state. True emotional independence requires the ability to forgive and release negative emotions, allowing you to move forward with clarity.

How to Avoid It:

Acknowledge the emotion behind the grudge, then choose to release it. Forgiveness doesn't mean excusing someone's behavior—it's about freeing yourself from the emotional burden. Reclaim your peace by focusing on growth and healing instead of lingering on past hurts.

3. Blaming Circumstances Instead of Owning Your Reactions

It's easy to blame external circumstances for your emotional state. You may think, "If only this hadn't happened, I'd feel better" or "If that person hadn't said that, I wouldn't be upset." This trap shifts responsibility for your emotions onto the outside world, rather than taking full ownership of your reactions.

Why This Is a Trap:

When you blame circumstances, you give away your power. The truth is, you can't control everything that happens to you, but you can control how you respond. By owning your reactions, you take control of your emotional state, regardless of external events.

How to Avoid It:

Recognize when you're blaming external circumstances. Shift your perspective by asking yourself, "What can I control here?" or "How can I respond in a way that aligns with my values?" Taking responsibility for your reactions allows you to maintain emotional control, no matter what's happening around you.

4. The Need for Constant Emotional Validation

Another trap of emotional dependence is the need for constant reassurance from others. Seeking emotional validation can manifest as a constant need for people to check in with you, reassure you, or offer support. While seeking support is natural, depending on it too much can leave you emotionally dependent on others' opinions.

Why This Is a Trap:

When you rely too much on emotional validation from others, you surrender control over your emotional state. You may struggle to make decisions or take action without looking for external approval. Emotional independence comes from trusting your own resilience and validating your feelings internally.

How to Avoid It:

Rather than constantly seeking reassurance, begin practicing self-reliance. Check in with yourself and recognize that your feelings are valid, regardless of others' opinions. This process will help you reduce emotional dependence and build stronger internal resilience.

Why This Changes Everything

Emotional independence is more than just a personal development tool it is the key to long-term success, inner peace, and influence in every area of life. When you master emotional independence, you stop allowing external circumstances to control your internal state. You take ownership of your emotions, responses, and actions, leading to a life of stability, purpose, and empowerment.

1. Toxic People Lose Their Power Over You

One of the most liberating aspects of emotional independence is that toxic people lose their power over you. When you rely on external validation, criticism, or approval from others, you give them emotional power over your state of mind. But when you manage your emotions independently, others' opinions no longer hold the same sway over you.

2. Setbacks Feel Like Detours, Not Dead Ends

Life is filled with unexpected challenges, and setbacks are inevitable. However, emotional independence allows you to view setbacks as detours, not dead ends. Rather than seeing obstacles as reasons to quit, you see them as opportunities for growth, learning, and resilience.

3. You Stop Chasing Validation, Which Frees You to Focus on Purpose

The constant need for external validation is one of the most exhausting emotional dependencies. When you stop seeking validation from others, you free yourself to focus on your purpose. Emotional independence allows you to focus on what matters most whether it's building your career, improving relationships, or pursuing personal goals—without seeking approval from the outside world.

4. Leadership Sharpened—People Trust Those Who Remain Calm Under Pressure

As a leader, your emotional state directly impacts your team's performance. When you remain calm under pressure, you set the emotional tone for your team. This is one of the most powerful aspects of emotional independence: leading by example. People trust leaders who are steady, decisive, and clear-headed even in times of stress.

5. Your Peace Becomes Portable

The most powerful aspect of emotional independence is that your peace becomes portable. No matter where you are or what's happening around you, you can carry your emotional peace with you. You are no longer at the mercy of external circumstances to feel calm and centered. Instead, your emotional state is self-contained, making you impervious to life's fluctuations.

The Emotional Tracking Drill

To begin mastering emotional independence, dedicate one week to tracking one emotion you frequently struggle with anger, worry, impatience, or anxiety. Use the following structure to document each instance:

- **The Trigger:**
  What caused the emotional reaction? Was it a situation, a person, or a thought?

- **Your Initial Impulse:**
  What was your first emotional reaction or impulse? Did you feel the urge to lash out, withdraw, or feel defeated?

- **The Action You Chose Instead:**
  How did you respond consciously? Did you pause, breathe, reframe the situation, or take a grounding action (e.g., journaling, walking)?

At the end of the week, you will have a clearer understanding of how often you experience this emotion, what triggers it, and how successfully you apply emotional independence strategies.

Why This Drill is Essential

This drill offers real-time feedback on your emotional responses. Rather than waiting for a major emotional event to disrupt your peace, you actively track and reflect on your emotional behavior. It makes emotional independence measurable and highlights areas for improvement.

Mastering emotional independence is the quiet superpower of modern life. In a world where technology, media, and society constantly pull at your attention and emotions, those who stay grounded rise above the noise. The reactive remain at its mercy, while those with emotional independence remain anchored, even in turbulence.

Your challenge is simple but lifelong: train your emotional muscles daily. Focus on building small victories, anticipate your emotional triggers, and lead with calm strength. When life's storms come—and they will—you'll stand unshaken. This is the power of emotional independence: becoming the anchor, no matter what life throws at you.

Advanced Traps of Emotional Dependence

One of the most overlooked traps of emotional dependence lies in ambition. Many believe they are working toward their personal goals, yet if the drive behind them stems from a need for external validation or approval, then emotional dependence is still in play.

Ask yourself: Would I still pursue this goal if no one knew I achieved it? Would I still choose this path if no one clapped? True emotional independence lies in the ability to answer yes to these questions, regardless of external feedback. When your drive comes from internal purpose, external validation no longer dictates your success.

Expanding Your Daily Practices

As discussed, grounding habits like meditation, journaling, prayer, and exercise are essential. To take this further, integrate them into an Emotional Conditioning Circuit:

- Start your day with five minutes of silence or deep breathing before engaging with technology.
- Take micro-breaks every hour to check in with your emotions and reset.
- End your day with a brief reflection; write down where you succeeded in controlling your reactions and where you could improve.

Repeated daily, this routine will begin to rewire your nervous system, gradually making steadiness your default emotional response.

Closing Charge

The storms of life are guaranteed; economic downturns, betrayals, loss, unexpected change. The question is not whether they will come, but whether you will stand or fall when they arrive. Emotional independence does not make the storms disappear, but it ensures that they never capsize you.

Carry this with you: be the anchor, and others will find stability through you. In a world built on chaos, your steadiness will become your greatest power.

Practical Steps to Internal Over External

Self-Awareness:

Begin by noticing your emotional triggers. When you are aware of what causes certain emotions, you can interrupt the emotional response before it escalates into a reaction. Keep track of situations where your emotions overwhelm you and take time to reflect on them.

Pause and Breathe:

When you feel a strong emotional reaction coming on, pause and take several deep breaths. This moment of pause gives you space to interrupt the emotional flood and create room for a more thoughtful response.

Reframe the Situation:

When faced with challenges, ask yourself, "What's another way to see this?" Shifting your perspective allows you to reframe the situation and choose a response that serves you. The mind can't hold two dominant interpretations at once, so choose the one that keeps you calm and aligned with your principles.

Commit to Personal Responsibility:

Acknowledge that how you respond is your responsibility. While you can't control the actions of others, you have full control over your response. Own your reactions and recognize that every emotional response is a choice you make.

CHAPTER

5

The Power of Decision-Making: Leading with Clarity Under Pressure.

The Weight of Decisions

Leadership is defined by decisions, not titles. The most crucial moments of leadership come when you are faced with pressure. Every decision you make ripples through your team, your organization, and even your personal life. People don't seek the loudest or most charismatic leader in times of crisis—they look for the one who can decide clearly and confidently, even when uncertainty looms.

The ability to act decisively in times of crisis can be the deciding factor between success and failure. However, decision-making in leadership carries weight. A poor decision can be corrected, but indecision is more dangerous. The consequences of inaction can erode trust, disrupt momentum, and create confusion among your team.

When you hesitate to make a choice, the team loses direction. The longer you delay, the more external factors control the narrative, leading to chaos. As a leader, hesitation is a greater danger than a wrong decision. Even if a decision turns out imperfectly, the act of deciding with conviction inspires confidence. A leader who demonstrates clarity guided by principles moves forward, even if the steps are not perfectly aligned.

Effective leaders make decisions with certainty, without sacrificing quality. Decisiveness isn't about acting recklessly, but about understanding the stakes, evaluating available information, and moving forward with purpose. The ability to decide, even when the path is uncertain, is the true test of leadership. Leaders who can act with clarity in uncertain times create trust, stability, and momentum that empower their teams to advance with confidence.

Principles of Decisive Leadership

Effective leadership hinges on the ability to make decisions that align with your core principles, not emotions or convenience. True leaders recognize that decision-making isn't about making perfect choices, but about acting with clarity and conviction. To lead with clarity under pressure, you must rely on guiding principles that keep you grounded and focused, no matter what chaos surrounds you.

In this section, we'll break down the core principles of decisive leadership. These principles will help you prioritize clarity, balance urgency with careful thought, build predictability, and take full responsibility for your actions—successes and failures alike.

1. Clarity Over Certainty

As a leader, you'll rarely have all the information needed to make the "perfect" decision. Certainty is often an illusion, particularly in complex situations. Waiting for absolute certainty can paralyze you in indecision. Instead, prioritize clarity; the ability to identify key factors and make a decision based on the best available information at the time.

Why This Works:

Clarity allows you to act with purpose, guiding you to prioritize what matters and move forward with conviction. While waiting for certainty may lead to stagnation, clarity propels you toward progress. A leader who seeks clarity will act, even when the path forward is unclear, building momentum along the way.

2. Speed Matters, But So Does Timing

Decisiveness is often associated with speed, but speed without thought can lead to rash decisions and poor outcomes. The key is balancing urgency with deliberate thought. Some decisions require swift action, while others benefit from patience and strategic consideration.

Why This Works:

Knowing when to act quickly and when to take more time allows you to navigate decisions wisely. Balancing speed and timing ensure that your decisions are both effective and well-thought-out.

3. Consistency Creates Predictability

Leaders don't need to be flawless, but they must be consistent. Consistency builds trust. When leaders make decisions based on stable principles, their actions become predictable. This predictability fosters confidence among team members.

Why This Works:

Consistency aligns actions with core values, creating stability. When teams know what to expect from their leader, it reduces anxiety and increases trust and buy-in.

4. Responsibility, Not Blame

Leaders take full responsibility for their decisions, whether they lead to success or failure. Blame undermines trust and damages credibility. Instead, owning outcomes even if they're less than ideal builds authority and respect.

Why This Works:

Taking responsibility demonstrates integrity and accountability. Leaders who own their decisions create a culture of ownership within their teams, inspiring others to take responsibility for their roles.

Frameworks for Decision-Making

As a leader, the ability to make well-informed decisions especially in high-pressure situations sets you apart. While intuition and experience are important, structured decision-making frameworks can help you eliminate emotional biases and gain clarity. These frameworks provide a clear, systematic approach to assess risks, opportunities, and potential outcomes, ensuring decisions are aligned with your values and goals.

In this section, we'll explain five decision-making frameworks that will guide you to navigate complex situations with confidence and precision.

1. The Values Filter

The Values Filter is a simple but powerful tool to ensure that your decisions are aligned with your core values. It helps you maintain integrity and make decisions consistent with your long-term vision, regardless of external pressures.

How to Use It:

Before making a decision, ask yourself:

- Does this decision align with my core values?
- Is this choice consistent with the long-term goals I've set for myself or my organization?
- Will this decision strengthen or erode the trust and credibility I've built with others?

Why This Works:

The Values Filter keeps you grounded and ensures that your decisions align with the bigger picture. It helps you avoid being swayed by short-term gains or external pressures, allowing you to make choices that reinforce your principles.

2. Second-Order Thinking

Second-order thinking encourages you to think beyond immediate consequences and consider the long-term impact of your decisions. By evaluating both short-term and long-term outcomes, you make decisions that prevent future problems.

How to Use It:

Ask yourself:

- What are the immediate consequences of this decision?
- What will the longer-term effects be?
- How will this decision impact the future; 6 months, 1 year, 5 years from now?

Why This Works:

Second-order thinking helps you avoid reactive decisions and encourages proactive planning. This framework ensures that your choices are well thought-out and sustainable, rather than quick fixes that could create bigger issues down the road.

3. The 80% Rule

Perfectionism often leads to paralysis by analysis. The 80% Rule encourages you to make decisions when you have enough clarity usually around 80% instead of waiting for 100% certainty. This rule helps you maintain momentum and avoid missed opportunities due to over-analysis.

How to Use It:

Ask yourself:

- Do I have enough information to make a decision?
- Is waiting for 100% certainty slowing progress?

Why This Works:

The 80% Rule encourages you to act, even when you don't have all the answers. Perfection is often an illusion, and decisions made with 80% clarity can still lead to great outcomes. Moving forward with confidence builds momentum, even if the decision isn't perfect.

4. Risk vs. Opportunity Mapping

The Risk vs. Opportunity Mapping framework helps you weigh the potential risks of taking action against the risks of inaction. This decision-making tool ensures that you don't get paralyzed by fear or hesitation, but instead, act strategically.

How to Use It:

Create two columns:

- Risks if I Act: What are the potential consequences of taking action?
- Risks if I Don't Act: What will happen if I do nothing? How will the situation worsen?

Why This Works:

By mapping out both sides of the decision, you get a clear picture of the risks involved. This helps you avoid the trap of inaction and take decisive steps, even when the future is uncertain.

5. Red Teaming

Red Teaming involves inviting a trusted colleague or team member to challenge your assumptions and test your decision before finalizing it. This helps uncover blind spots and ensures more well-rounded decision-making.

How to Use It:

Designate someone you trust to review your decision and provide feedback. Ask them to:

- Challenge your assumptions.
- Identify weaknesses or gaps in your logic.
- Provide alternative perspectives.

Why This Works:

By incorporating external feedback, Red Teaming helps you identify weaknesses in your thinking and make more informed decisions. This process reduces the risk of making unilateral decisions without considering other viewpoints.

Common Traps in Leadership Decisions

Effective leadership requires the ability to make decisions that drive progress. However, even experienced leaders can fall into subtle traps that hinder effective decision-making. These traps are often driven by emotions, biases, and overthinking, leading to hesitation or poor choices. Recognizing these traps is essential for making decisions grounded in clarity and aligned with your values.

1. Analysis Paralysis

Analysis paralysis occurs when a leader overthinks a decision to the point of inaction. It's important to gather enough information to make informed decisions, but spending too much time analyzing can delay progress and create unnecessary anxiety.

2. Emotional Hijacking

Emotions such as anger, fear, or pride can cloud judgment, leading to impulsive decisions. Leaders who allow emotions to dictate their decisions risk making choices they later regret.

3. Popularity Over Principle

Leaders sometimes fall into the trap of making decisions to please everyone or avoid conflict. This approach undermines authenticity and dilutes integrity.

4. Overconfidence Bias

Leaders who are overconfident in their abilities or decisions risk underestimating risks and failing to seek alternative perspectives.

5. Delegation Avoidance

Leaders who hesitate to delegate decisions risk bottlenecks, burnout, and missed growth opportunities for their teams. While taking ownership of decisions is important, avoiding delegation undermines team development.

Case Studies in Decisive Leadership

Decision-making in leadership is often tested under pressure. Here are some examples of leaders navigating challenges by applying practical decision-making frameworks. These case studies showcase how structured frameworks help leaders remain grounded and confident under pressure.

1. Business Leader in Crisis: Principle-Based Decision Making

A business leader faces a financial challenge when revenues drop unexpectedly. They must decide between drastic cost-cutting measures, such as laying off staff, or adjusting company-wide operations. The decision must align with their core value of employee loyalty.

Decision-Making Framework Applied:

Values Filter: The leader evaluates the decision against the company's core value of employee loyalty. The decision is made to implement pay cuts across the company, including executive salaries, rather than layoffs.

Outcome:

This decision allowed the business to weather the financial downturn while preserving workforce morale and loyalty, reinforcing the company's long-term vision.

2. Security Professional: Decision Making in High-Pressure Situations

A security manager notices suspicious activity at a facility entrance. They must decide whether to confront the person immediately or wait for backup. In this high-stress moment, the Risk vs. Opportunity Mapping framework is applied.

Decision-Making Framework Applied:

Risk vs. Opportunity Mapping: The security manager decides that waiting for backup reduces the risk of confrontation escalating. The decision is made to call for backup and secure the scene.

Outcome:

The decision resulted in a controlled situation without violence. The framework ensured a methodical response to a high-pressure situation.

3. Military Leader: Speed Over Perfection

A military leader faces a critical operational decision, whether to wait for more intelligence or act immediately with incomplete data. The leader applies second-order thinking to weigh the risks of waiting.

Decision-Making Framework Applied:

Second-Order Thinking: By acting quickly, the military leader gains the initiative and completes the mission successfully, despite imperfect data.

Outcome:

The decision ensured the team remained proactive, preventing potential delays in a high-stakes operation.

4. Entrepreneur: Weighing Risk and Reward

An entrepreneur is offered an investment that promises rapid growth but would dilute control over their company. The entrepreneur uses second-order thinking to consider long-term consequences before deciding to decline the offer.

Decision-Making Framework Applied:

Second-Order Thinking: The entrepreneur chooses long-term control over short-term gain, ensuring that the company remains aligned with their vision.

Outcome:

The decision leads to more sustainable growth and better alignment with the company's core values.

5. Law Enforcement Leader: Leading with Clarity Under Pressure

A police officer arrives at a chaotic accident scene. The officer must decide whether to assist the injured, manage traffic, or secure the scene. The officer applies the Prioritization Framework to focus on the most urgent need.

Decision-Making Framework Applied:

Prioritization Framework: The officer secures the scene first to ensure safety, then assists with the injured and directs traffic.

Outcome:

By prioritizing safety first, the officer restores order quickly, ensuring minimal additional risk or injury.

Exercise 1: The 60-Second Rule (Training Decisiveness)

Purpose:

This drill trains you to act swiftly and confidently, honing your decision-making ability in both low and high-stakes situations.

How to Use It:

- Set a 60-second timer for decisions on low-stakes tasks: scheduling, email responses, small meetings. The goal is to make the decision quickly and without second-guessing.
- Reflect briefly on whether your choice aligns with your core values and goals, and make a quick decision within the time limit.

Reflection Prompt:

- When did you hesitate recently on a decision? Can you identify a small decision where you could have acted with more clarity?

Exercise 2: The Worst-Case Visualization (Facing Fear)

Principle:

Fear often paralyzes leaders, but the key to overcoming it is to confront the worst possible outcome. By acknowledging and visualizing the worst-case scenario, you gain control over the situation and reduce fear.

How to Use It:

- When faced with a difficult decision, ask yourself: "What's the worst that could happen if I make this choice?"
- Write it down, acknowledge the fear, and ask yourself: "Can I handle this?" Most of the time, the answer is yes, and action becomes easier.

Reflection Prompt:

- Reflect on a recent decision where fear played a role. How can you visualize the worst-case outcome and use that to reduce fear in future decisions?

Exercise 3: The Daily Prioritization Drill (Focus on What Matters)

Principle:

Leaders must prioritize what matters most. By recognizing and focusing on your top priority, you train yourself to make decisions based on the most critical issue at hand.

How to Use It:

- Every morning, identify one key decision you must make that day.
- Prioritize it above everything else, ensuring you allocate time and energy to this decision before allowing smaller distractions to take over.

Reflection Prompt:

- What is the most important decision you need to make today? Are you focused on it, or are smaller distractions pulling your attention?

Exercise 4: The "First Priority" Drill (Clear Focus Under Pressure)

Principle:

In moments of overwhelm, focus is essential. The "First Priority" drill ensures that you cut through the mental clutter and focus on the most important task at hand.

How to Use It:

- When facing a difficult decision or stressful situation, ask yourself: "What is the one thing I need to focus on right now?"
- Write it down and make it your top priority. Tackle this first before anything else.

Reflection Prompt:

- In your next challenging moment, ask: "What's the single most important thing I need to focus on?" Notice how this shifts your perspective and empowers you to act decisively.

Exercise 5: The Three Options Rule (Expanding Your Choices)

Principle:

Sticking to one approach often limits decision-making. By generating three distinct options, you break free from tunnel vision and open yourself to more creative, effective solutions.

How to Use It:

Before deciding, ask yourself: "What are three options I could consider?"

- The Obvious: The conventional or standard approach.
- The Risky: A bold approach that carries risk but potentially higher rewards.
- The Creative: An unconventional solution that requires out-of-the-box thinking.

Reflection Prompt:

- Consider a decision you made recently. Did you generate multiple options, or did you choose the obvious path? How would considering more options change the outcome?

Each of these drills is designed to strengthen your decision-making muscle in low-stakes environments so that when the pressure is on, you're equipped to make clear, confident choices. Consistent practice with these tools will not only improve your decision-making but also build your leadership clarity.

1. How do I typically respond to high-pressure decisions?

Purpose: This prompt helps you assess how you handle stress and pressure in decision-making scenarios.

Reflection Focus:

- Are you calm and composed, or do you tend to rush when facing uncertainty?
- Reflect on a recent situation where you had to make a decision under pressure. How did you feel during that time?
- Identify what you did well and areas where you could have improved your response.

Action Step:

Think about a high-pressure decision you made recently. Review your emotional state and actions. Could you have taken a different approach for a better outcome?

2. What is the most recent decision I made, and what framework did I use to make it?

Purpose: This reflection focuses on ensuring you are using decision-making frameworks to guide your choices.

Reflection Focus:

- What frameworks or principles did you use? For example, Values Filter, Second-Order Thinking, or Risk vs. Opportunity Mapping.

- Did you make your decision with clarity, or were there any moments of hesitation, emotional hijacking, or overthinking?

Action Step:

Take note of the decision frameworks you are using daily and ask if they align with your principles and values. Revisit any decisions where you experienced doubt or emotional bias.

3. When I hesitate, what's the underlying reason?

Purpose: Identifying the root causes of hesitation helps you address the emotional or psychological barriers to effective decision-making.

Reflection Focus:

- Do you hesitate due to fear of failure, perfectionism, or a lack of confidence?
- Identify any patterns in your hesitation and assess whether these causes are rational or internally imposed.

Action Step:

Next time you hesitate, take a moment to pause and identify the reason behind your hesitation. Challenge your fears and take action, focusing on what's important, not perfect.

4. How can I practice making quicker decisions?

Purpose: This prompt aims to build your decisiveness by identifying opportunities to practice faster decision-making in low-stakes situations.

Reflection Focus:

- Are there smaller, daily decisions where you can practice making faster choices to build confidence?
- Try the 60-Second Rule: Start with minor decisions like scheduling or meal choices to build your decisiveness.

Action Step:

Set a timer and make decisions quickly for smaller daily tasks. Assess how this practice builds momentum and improves your ability to decide swiftly in more significant situations.

5. What does my decision-making reveal about my leadership?

Purpose: This reflection helps you evaluate how your decision-making style influences your leadership effectiveness.

Reflection Focus:

- How does your style impact those you lead?
- Are your decisions aligned with your core values and the overall mission of your team or organization?
- Reflect on how your decisions shape your credibility and influence as a leader.

Action Step:

Consider a recent decision. How did it affect your team's trust in your leadership? Write down ways to strengthen your decision-making process to align more closely with your values and your team's needs.

6. Which decision-making principle do I need to apply more often?

Purpose: To help you identify areas of improvement in your decision-making process, especially in applying core principles consistently.

Reflection Focus:

- From the principles discussed (e.g., clarity, second-order thinking, responsibility), which one do you find most difficult to implement regularly?
- Set a goal to apply that principle more consciously over the next week.

Action Step:

Choose one decision-making principle that feels challenging and intentionally apply it to a decision you face this week. Reflect on how focusing on that principle helps you make more aligned, effective choices.

Closing Words

As explained in this chapter, decision-making is the cornerstone of leadership. Every decision you make whether minor or major directly impacts your team, organization, or family, and shapes the culture you create. Leadership is not defined by the title you hold, but by the decisions you make in the face of challenges and uncertainty.

In moments of pressure, it's not the loudest voice that leads but the one that can make decisions with clarity and conviction. The most effective leaders are not flawless; they are those who make decisions grounded in purpose and principles. True leadership is about the ability to decide swiftly, take decisive action, and course-correct when necessary. It's about taking ownership of the consequences, whether the outcome is success or failure.

When faced with uncertainty, remember that indecision creates confusion. It stifles momentum, breeds doubt, and erodes trust. On the contrary, decisiveness fosters confidence, strengthens trust, and establishes clarity. The ability to act, even when the path is unclear, separates great leaders from those who merely occupy leadership roles.

Now it's time to put everything into practice. The frameworks, principles, and drills we've discussed are not just theoretical they are tools designed to help you lead with confidence and clarity. The true power of decision-making lies in your ability to consistently apply these tools in your daily life and leadership.

Your challenge is to implement these frameworks as you navigate both small everyday decisions and high-pressure, high-stakes moments. Whether in routine choices or moments of crisis, use the decision-making tools you've learned to guide your actions. Practice the 60-second rule, worst-case visualization, and reflection drills. Allow your leadership to serve as a model of decisiveness, clarity, and principled action.

As you move forward, remember: your decisions shape the culture and momentum of your team. Each choice carries weight, not just in the moment, but for the long-term success and growth of those you lead.

Your leadership is defined by your ability to make decisions with clarity and conviction and to lead by example. Practice these principles, and you will see your leadership evolve into a foundation of trust, confidence, and impact. The decisions you make today determine the trajectory of your leadership tomorrow.

Strategic Vision and Execution: Turning Ideas into Reality.

Why Vision Matters

A leader without vision is simply a manager of tasks. Vision is what makes leadership meaningful; it's the force that drives teams and organizations toward a greater purpose, one that resonates deeply with every member of the group. Without vision, leadership feels like a series of disconnected tasks—a checklist of to-dos that never seem to build toward something larger. But with vision, every action is part of a mission, a greater goal that provides clarity and direction.

People don't rally around checklists. They rally around purpose. A compelling vision answers the question every follower quietly asks: "Where are we going, and why should I follow you?" Leaders who are solely focused on task management fail to inspire their teams, because they have nothing to offer beyond immediate, transactional goals. But leaders with a vision don't just manage, they lead.

Vision vs. Execution

However, having a vision is not enough. A leader may have a grand vision for the future, but without the ability to execute, that vision remains a dream unrealized and disconnected from the day-to-day realities of the team. This is where many leaders fail. They may be able to paint an inspiring picture of the future, but they struggle to break it down into actionable steps that move the team forward.

On the flip side, execution without vision leads to burnout. Teams can work tirelessly on tasks, but without a clear direction, the work becomes meaningless, and the motivation fades. Leaders who fail to connect their teams' work to a larger vision often find themselves surrounded by busy people who are not really getting anywhere.

The magic happens when vision meets execution. A vision gives the team a compelling reason to keep moving forward, even when the work gets hard. It provides a sense of purpose, while execution provides the structure and discipline to turn that purpose into reality. Together, they create a roadmap for success one that aligns the team's efforts with a greater goal and ensures that each step forward is a step toward a meaningful future.

Why Vision Inspires Action

The power of a clear vision lies in its ability to inspire. A well-crafted vision is simple, authentic, and aligned with values. It paints a picture of the future that excites the team, motivating them to take consistent action toward that goal. But to inspire, the vision must be clear. It must be something everyone can understand, repeat, and believe in. If a leader cannot express their vision in a clear, simple sentence, then it is likely to be misunderstood or ignored.

Principles of Strategic Vision

Strategic vision is the compass that guides a leader and their team toward a successful future. A vision provides the clarity needed to make consistent decisions, align efforts, and drive collective momentum. The principles that underpin an effective strategic vision must go beyond theory and inspire action. These principles ensure that the vision is not just aspirational, but actionable, sustainable, and deeply connected to the daily work of the team.

1. Clarity Over Complexity

A strategic vision is only valuable if it can be easily understood and acted upon. When crafting a vision, simplicity should always take precedence over complexity. Vision should not be laden with jargon, abstract statements, or convoluted language that leaves people confused. Instead, the vision must be clear and simple enough for anyone—whether a new team member or a child—to articulate it in a single sentence. When the message is clear, it inspires confidence and gives people a direction they can follow.

2. Alignment with Core Values

A vision that isn't grounded in the organization's core values is unlikely to be sustained. Values are the foundation upon which vision rests, and they serve as an anchor in turbulent times. A leader must ensure that the vision flows directly from these values, as this connection makes the vision not only more authentic but also more enduring.

3. Foresight and Adaptability

A rigid, unyielding vision can become outdated as the world shifts around it. While foresight is critical i.e anticipating changes, trends, and challenges, it must be balanced with adaptability. The ability to pivot and adjust execution without abandoning the ultimate destination is the hallmark of effective leadership. Leaders who can see around corners and adjust to new circumstances without losing sight of the overall goal are best equipped to lead their teams through periods of uncertainty.

4. Communicated Relentlessly

A vision that is stated once and then forgotten is a vision that will fail to inspire. For a vision to truly take root within a team, it must be communicated relentlessly. This means integrating it into every aspect of the organization—every meeting, every decision, every interaction. Leaders must weave the vision into their messaging so that it becomes part of the organization's culture, not just a statement on a wall or a website.

5. Connected to Execution

A vision without execution is simply a dream. To make a vision tangible, it must be connected to the work being done on the ground. Leaders who inspire but never implement breed cynicism. The true test of a vision is whether it survives contact with reality. Leaders must turn vision into actionable steps, showing how each task or decision contributes to the realization of the larger goal.

Principles of Strategic Vision

Strategic vision is the backbone of effective leadership. Without it, a leader is simply managing tasks, rather than inspiring action toward a shared goal. Vision serves as the guiding light, giving clarity and direction to every decision and step taken by the team. But a vision must be grounded in key principles to ensure its impactful and actionable. Below are the core principles of strategic vision, designed to guide you in creating and leading with a vision that inspires and propels your team forward.

1. Clarity Over Complexity

A vision must be simple and clear. It should be a statement that anyone whether a new team member or a leader can understand and recite easily. Complexity often breeds confusion, while clarity empowers action.

Why This Works:

A clear, concise vision makes it easier for people to understand the "why" behind their actions, giving them a sense of purpose. When your vision is simple, it becomes accessible to everyone, ensuring that every member of your team is aligned and working toward a common goal. When you strip away complexity, you invite clarity, which leads to stronger decision-making and cohesive team effort.

Example:

Instead of a complex vision like "Develop a market-leading product that integrates with multiple systems to provide an intuitive user experience," consider something simpler like: "To create the most user-friendly product that seamlessly integrates into any workflow." This simplified vision still conveys the key goal but is easier for your team to remember and rally behind.

2. Alignment with Core Values

A vision must be rooted in the core values of the organization or team. If the vision is detached from the values that define the group, it will lack authenticity and will be difficult to implement when challenges arise.

Why This Works:

People do not just follow a vision; they follow a vision that aligns with their values. A vision grounded in shared values feels natural and unifying, which builds trust and engagement. When the vision and values are in sync, the team can weather challenges because they are working toward something that resonates deeply with their core beliefs.

Example:

If your organization values "collaboration" and "innovation," ensure that your vision reflects these. For instance, "To foster a collaborative and innovative work environment that empowers teams to push the boundaries of what's possible." This speaks directly to the values your team holds dear, reinforcing the collective mission.

3. Foresight and Adaptability

While a vision must remain focused on the end goal, it also needs to remain flexible. The external world is constantly changing, and a rigid vision can quickly become irrelevant. Leaders who can balance foresight with adaptability are the ones who remain successful in ever-evolving environments.

Why This Works:

Foresight allows you to anticipate shifts, while adaptability ensures you can adjust your approach without losing sight of the end goal. By embracing change and making adjustments as needed, you keep your vision alive and relevant, ensuring the team stays on track even when circumstances change.

Example:

Consider a company that has a vision to lead in sustainable fashion. As new materials and technologies become available, the company adapts its processes to incorporate these innovations without losing sight of its core mission. This balance of foresight and adaptability ensures the company stays at the forefront of its industry while remaining aligned with its original vision.

4. Communicated Relentlessly

A vision must be communicated frequently and consistently. Saying it once is not enough; leaders must weave the vision into every interaction, meeting, and decision. The more a vision is communicated, the more it becomes ingrained in the culture.

Why This Works:

When a vision is communicated consistently, it becomes a part of the organization's DNA. It guides daily decisions, helps shape company culture, and ensures that everyone in the team is aligned with the larger purpose. Communication is not about repetition; it's about ensuring that the vision is always top-of-mind.

Example:

In a weekly meeting, the leader might open with a reminder of the vision: "Remember, we're here to innovate and improve the lives of our customers with our technology. Every decision we make should reflect that." This constant reinforcement keeps the team connected to the larger purpose.

5. Connected to Execution

A vision is only valuable if it translates into action. Leaders who inspire but fail to implement risk breeding cynicism and disengagement. The vision must connect to the day-to-day work, ensuring that every task, no matter how small, is contributing to the larger goal.

Why This Works:

Execution turns a vision into reality. Leaders who connect vision to tangible actions ensure that every team member understands how their work contributes to the greater mission. This alignment of effort and vision drives consistent progress and builds momentum.

Example:

If the vision is "To become the world leader in renewable energy," every strategic decision, from resource allocation to team structure, should reflect this goal. The leader must break down the vision into concrete steps and actions that align the team's efforts with the larger mission.

The principles of strategic vision are not just theoretical, they are actionable guidelines that help you lead with clarity, purpose, and impact. By focusing on clarity, aligning with core values, adapting to change, and communicating consistently, you will inspire and motivate your team to move toward a shared goal. Execution ensures that your vision stays alive in the day-to-day work, and when these principles come together, they create a powerful roadmap to success.

Common Traps in Visionary Leadership

1. Confusing Vision with Fantasy

A vision should be ambitious, but it must also be realistic. Leaders can fall into the trap of creating grand, unrealistic visions that can demotivate their teams. The key is to ensure the vision remains achievable and grounded in reality.

When a vision is seen as an unrealistic fantasy, it loses its credibility and causes frustration among the team. Visionary leadership should focus on inspiring the team while ensuring the vision is pragmatic and attainable.

2. Neglecting Execution

Vision without execution is simply a dream. Visionary leaders often make the mistake of focusing too much on the vision while neglecting the steps required to bring it to life.

True visionary leadership requires attention to the details and consistent action. Execution provides the framework for the vision, ensuring it doesn't remain a distant ideal but becomes a tangible reality. Leaders must strike a balance between dreaming big and ensuring that their vision is translated into concrete actions.

3. Failure to Adapt

A vision that is too rigid can become obsolete. Successful leaders balance foresight with the ability to adapt. The world is constantly changing, and what seemed like a strong vision can become outdated if it's not flexible.

Visionary leadership involves maintaining a clear destination while remaining adaptable in the approach. Leaders must evolve their strategies based on new information or changing circumstances without abandoning the core vision. Adaptability is crucial to ensuring the vision remains relevant.

4. Overcomplicating Communication

The power of a vision lies in its simplicity. When leaders use complex language, jargon, or lengthy explanations, the vision becomes difficult for the team to grasp and rally behind.

A strong vision should be simple, clear, and easy to communicate. When the vision is overcomplicated, it loses its ability to inspire and guide. Leaders must ensure that the vision is easily understood by all, regardless of their role or experience. Clarity is key.

5. Delegating Vision

The vision is the leader's responsibility, and it cannot be delegated. When leaders rely on others to communicate the vision, they risk losing its authenticity and the personal connection that is vital for engaging the team.

The leader must take ownership of the vision and ensure it is communicated consistently across all levels. Direct engagement with the vision ensures it remains personal, genuine, and aligned with the leader's actions and values.

Case Studies in Visionary Leadership

Case Study 1: The Tech Innovator

A startup founder envisioned making personal computing accessible to everyday households at a time when computers were niche and expensive. Rather than attempting to solve everything at once, the founder broke the vision into small, achievable milestones: designing user-friendly interfaces, developing compact and efficient hardware, and ensuring affordability for mass markets. Each milestone was tested and refined based on feedback, keeping the process grounded in reality while moving steadily toward the larger goal.

Case Study 2: The Military Campaign

A general tasked with stabilizing a conflict-ridden region understood that victory on the battlefield alone would not ensure long-term security. The ultimate goal was local communities capable of operating independently without constant external support. To achieve this, the general implemented backward planning: training local security forces, establishing infrastructure, and securing key supply lines, each action aligned with the larger vision.

Case Study 3: The Corporate Turnaround

A struggling company faced the risk of bankruptcy, compounded by poor culture and declining customer trust. Rather than focusing solely on cost-cutting, the new CEO cast a vision: becoming the most trusted provider in the industry. She aligned every department with this goal—retraining customer service teams, improving operational transparency, and simplifying marketing messaging.

Case Study 4: The Sports Coach

A coach inherited a team with a history of poor performance. Instead of focusing solely on winning championships, he cast a vision of becoming "the hardest working team in the league." This vision was grounded in controllable behaviors: consistent effort, focus, and discipline in practice. Players could engage with the vision daily, which created buy-in and a culture of accountability.

Case Study 5:

The Government Reformer A newly elected leader inherited a government plagued by inefficiency and mistrust. Instead of promising vague "better policies," he cast a vision of "transparent government accessible to every citizen." He backed this with specific, tangible steps: digitizing records, reducing red tape, and holding open forums. Though critics mocked his simplicity, execution proved powerful. Within years, citizens felt more engaged, and public trust increased. The lesson: vision in leadership must be both clear and practical to break through resistance.

Case Study 6:

The Nonprofit Builder A nonprofit founder had almost no resources but envisioned transforming literacy in underserved communities. She cast a vision of "every child holding a book by age five." With little funding, she executed through partnerships — engaging volunteers, securing book donations, and creating pop-up reading programs. The vision's simplicity attracted supporters who shared the passion. Within a decade, the nonprofit grew nationally. The case shows that even with limited resources, a clear vision executed consistently draws momentum.

Lesson Learned

Vision is not about seeing every detail at once, it is about consistently moving toward a clear destination. Breaking the vision into manageable steps, tying it to controllable behaviors, and ensuring execution aligns with purpose are what turn ambitious ideas into reality. A clear, actionable vision inspires commitment, drives momentum, and creates lasting impact.

Drills for Leaders

1. The One-Sentence Vision Drill

A great vision is one that can be easily understood and communicated. The clarity of your vision is paramount to guiding the team effectively. If it takes more than a sentence to explain, it may not be clear enough.

How to Use It:

- Write your vision in one sentence – Aim to distill the vision into a clear, concise statement.
- Test it – Share the sentence with a colleague or team member and ask them to repeat it in their own words. If they can, it's likely clear. If not, simplify it further.

Why This Works:

This drill forces you to distill your vision into a single, powerful sentence, ensuring clarity. A clear, actionable vision is easier for your team to grasp and align with.

2. Backward Mapping Exercise

Once you have your clear vision, it's time to break it down into actionable steps. The Backward Mapping Exercise helps you reverse-engineer the vision, starting from the end goal and working backward to identify the necessary milestones and actions that lead to success.

How to Use It:

- Define your end state – What does success look like 3 years from now?
- Work backward – Identify the key milestones that need to be achieved along the way.
- Break milestones into smaller steps – Break those milestones down into quarterly or monthly goals.

Why This Works:

Backward mapping turns your vision into concrete actions. It provides a clear roadmap by identifying the necessary steps and ensuring that every action aligns with your ultimate goal.

3. Vision Repetition Habit

A vision needs to be constantly reinforced. This drill encourages you to make your vision part of your daily leadership routine and your team's culture.

How to Use It:

- Mention the vision daily – Ensure its part of every meeting and conversation with your team.
- Embed it in decision-making – Refer back to your vision when making important choices.
- Encourage your team – Invite your team to repeat the vision back to you, solidifying it in their minds.

Why This Works:

Without regular reinforcement, a vision can quickly fade into the background. The Vision Repetition Habit ensures the vision stays top-of-mind for both you and your team, helping actions stay aligned with the larger mission.

4. Distraction Elimination Drill

In a fast-paced world, distractions are inevitable. This drill helps you identify and remove tasks that don't align with your vision, allowing you to focus on what truly matters.

How to Use It:

- List current projects and priorities – Write down everything you're currently working on.
- Eliminate one project – Identify and remove one task that doesn't directly support your vision.
- Focus on what matters – Concentrate your efforts on projects that drive you closer to your goals.

Why This Works:

By eliminating distractions, you prioritize actions that move you closer to your vision. This habit helps build momentum and ensures focus on what truly matters for success.

5. Daily Execution Anchor

Execution is the key to bringing your vision to life. The Daily Execution Anchor drill helps you start each day with clarity by focusing on the one action that will move you closest to your vision.

How to Use It:

- Ask yourself each morning: What is the one most important action I can take today to move closer to the vision?
- Prioritize that action – Make sure to take that one action first, before other tasks distract you.

Why This Works:

By starting your day with focus on the most impactful task, you build momentum and avoid falling into the trap of busy work. This drill ensures that your daily actions are in alignment with your vision, promoting purposeful execution.

6. The Vision Cascade Drill

One of the most important aspects of leadership is ensuring that your vision is not only clear to you but also to those you lead. A vision that can't be clearly communicated and repeated by others is a vision that hasn't truly taken root within your team.

How to Use It:

Write down your one-sentence vision. Then, ask three people whether on your team or in your household—to explain your vision back to you in their own words.

If their answers vary, it indicates that the vision hasn't fully cascaded through the group.

Refine the message and communicate it again. Repeat the process until the essence of your vision remains consistent across different levels.

Why This Works:

True vision is not simply what the leader says, it's what others understand, remember, and repeat. This drill ensures that your vision has been communicated effectively and has permeated the entire team. When everyone can articulate the same vision, alignment is achieved, and collective effort is directed toward a common goal.

Reflection Prompts: Clarifying Your Vision and Aligning Actions

As a leader, regular reflection is crucial to assess whether your actions, decisions, and leadership are aligned with your vision. Use the following prompts to evaluate your progress, refine your approach, and ensure that every action you take is steering you closer to your goal.

1. Can I articulate my vision in one sentence right now?

Your vision should be clear, concise, and easy to communicate. If you cannot summarize it in a single sentence, it might need further refinement to ensure it's straightforward and memorable. Take a moment to craft your vision statement.

2. Do my daily actions align with my stated vision?

Every day presents opportunities to move closer to your vision. Reflect on whether your daily tasks, decisions, and interactions are aligned with your long-term goal. If not, identify where you might need to recalibrate.

3. What distractions currently pull me away from execution?

In a world full of noise, it's easy to become distracted by tasks that don't contribute to your vision. Identify which activities or people are pulling your focus away from what truly matters, and develop strategies to eliminate them.

4. How do I communicate vision — occasionally, or relentlessly?

Vision is only as powerful as its communication. Reflect on how frequently and effectively you communicate your vision to your team. Is it integrated into every conversation and decision? Or is it something that comes up only occasionally?

5. If my team acted only on what I repeat most often, what would they think the vision is?

Your actions and words shape your team's understanding of the vision. Reflect on whether you are consistently reinforcing the core elements of the vision. If your team were to act solely on your frequent messages, would their actions align with the vision you intend to communicate?

These prompts are designed to help you reflect deeply on your leadership approach and ensure that your actions and communication are fully aligned with your vision. Regular reflection enables you to make adjustments, keep your team focused, and drive continuous progress toward your long-term goals.

Closing: Vision That Touches the Ground

Vision without execution is fantasy. Execution without vision is exhaustion. Leadership requires both: the courage to declare where you are going, and the discipline to make it real.

When leaders connect vision to execution, they transform effort into meaning. People will sacrifice, innovate, and endure when they see the bigger picture. Vision answers why we work; execution answers how we win.

Your challenge is to craft a vision that is clear, credible, and deeply connected to your values—and then, turn that vision into daily execution. A leader who does this doesn't just set goals. They create movements.

Vision does more than guide today's actions, it sets the stage for the future. Great leaders are remembered less for their day-to-day decisions and more for the futures they made believable.

Take Martin Luther King Jr. for instance. When he declared, "I have a dream," he didn't hand out a strategic plan—he shared a vision that has inspired decades of execution across movements. Similarly, when Winston Churchill declared victory was inevitable during the darkest hours of World War II, he cast a vision that rallied nations. In both cases, the vision outlived the leader because it was simple, values-based, and closely connected to action.

Your leadership is measured not only by what you build, but by what endures after you're gone. Vision creates continuity beyond your presence. It becomes culture, legacy, and inheritance. Vision without execution dies with the leader, but vision connected to execution lives on as legacy.

Your task, therefore, is not only to define a destination but to embed it so deeply in others that they continue moving forward even when you are no longer leading.

The Lone Wolf Advantage: Self-Reliance as the First Step to Leadership

Why the Lone Wolf Matters?

Most people fear solitude. Silence often feels uncomfortable, and being alone can feel like being cut off from the world. However, true leadership begins when you no longer need the crowd to validate your path. The lone wolf is not about isolation but about independence. He learns to stand firm in solitude, to make decisions without waiting for others' approval, and to trust his instincts without external validation.

Leadership built on dependence is fragile. It's shaped by the opinions and approval of others, which can easily waver. In contrast, leadership built on self-reliance is unshakable. The lone wolf doesn't need permission from the pack. He stands firm, grounded in his own convictions. Before you can lead others, you must first prove you can lead yourself.

True leadership begins with the strength to move forward independently, even when no one else is. It's about cultivating the inner confidence to make decisions based on your values, not on the validation or approval of others.

The Psychology of Independence

The human brain is wired for connection. Throughout history, isolation often meant danger or even death. As social creatures, humans evolved to crave belonging, approval, and security within the group. This deep-seated need for validation is built into our neural architecture—whether through praise from others, likes on social media, or the applause we receive for our actions. However, in today's hyper-connected world, this natural craving is often exaggerated, leaving many people trapped by the constant need for external validation. This dependency on external sources for self-worth can limit growth and undermine the development of true self-reliance.

Self-reliance, however, requires a fundamental shift in how we view and train our minds. It's about rewiring our thought processes to rely on internal validation rather than seeking approval from the crowd.

1. Neuroplasticity and Solitude

One of the most powerful tools for cultivating self-reliance is solitude. While the idea of being alone may seem daunting to some, studies show that solitude can actually be a powerful catalyst for personal growth. Neuroscientifically, solitude enhances creativity, problem-solving, and mental clarity. This happens by quieting external noise, which allows the brain to strengthen neural connections in the prefrontal cortex, the area responsible for higher-order thinking, decision-making, and self-regulation. In moments of solitude, you begin to connect ideas more fluidly, gain new insights, and improve your cognitive flexibility.

In solitude, your brain is forced to rely on its internal resources, which strengthens both your capacity for independent thought and emotional resilience. The more you embrace moments of quiet reflection, the more you recondition your mind to function without the constant influence of external stimuli.

2. Dopamine and Independence

We live in a world driven by instant gratification. Social media, news cycles, and workplace feedback all serve as a source of quick dopamine hits—feel-good moments that reinforce our dependence on external validation. However, when you begin to embrace self-reliance, your brain starts rewiring itself to derive satisfaction from progress, discipline, and internal rewards.

This shift occurs gradually, but it's significant. Instead of relying on external praise to feel accomplished, you begin to derive dopamine from self-discipline and the satisfaction of your own efforts. For example, the sense of accomplishment you feel after completing a challenging task on your own, without external recognition, can begin to replace the fleeting dopamine hits that come from seeking approval.

3. Stress Resilience

Another critical aspect of developing self-reliance is learning to handle stress effectively. People who practice solitude regularly show lower cortisol reactivity, meaning they experience less physiological stress in the face of challenges. Why? Because solitude helps train the nervous system to operate more calmly and effectively under pressure. The lone wolf doesn't run from stress. Instead, he faces it head-on, learning to remain clear-headed even without the reassurance of external validation.

By regularly engaging in solitary practices like reflection, journaling, or even silent walks, you become more adept at managing stress, without the need to seek relief through external sources. This builds mental fortitude, allowing you to remain calm and focused when the world around you is chaotic.

Case Studies of the Lone Wolf

The journey to true self-reliance and strength often takes place in solitude. Throughout history, some of the most revered leaders, thinkers, and achievers found their power in moments of isolation. These case studies highlight how solitude, self-reliance, and independent thinking have been integral to the success of individuals who embodied the Lone Wolf mindset.

Marcus Aurelius: The Emperor's Private Reflection

Even as one of the most powerful men in history, Marcus Aurelius, the Roman Emperor, found strength in solitude. His leadership was not shaped by endless debates with advisers or the grand speeches to the public, but by his time spent alone in reflection.

Every day, he journaled in solitude writing not for an audience, but for himself. His thoughts were a collection of reminders, corrections, strategies, and reflections on how he could govern with wisdom and integrity. His famous Meditations are filled with passages where he wrestles with his own thoughts, finding clarity and wisdom through private reflection. This daily ritual of self-dialogue and introspection helped him maintain mental clarity and calm, even as he faced the burdens of ruling an empire.

Lesson: Marcus Aurelius teaches us that true wisdom and leadership often come from within. Solitude allowed him to cultivate a mindset of self-reliance and self-reflection, which in turn made him an effective and grounded leader.

Elon Musk: The Solitary Pioneer

Long before Tesla and SpaceX became household names, Elon Musk's vision for the future was mocked and doubted by many. At a critical time, when investors were pulling out and experts were skeptical, Musk chose to invest his own money into his ventures. He even went as far as to sleep on the factory floor at Tesla, pushing himself to work relentlessly toward his vision, even when others saw it as a lost cause.

Musk's ability to withstand the skepticism, ridicule, and uncertainty, and to remain focused on his long-term vision, is a testament to his Lone Wolf mentality. His willingness to stand alone in those formative years laid the foundation for the innovation and success that followed.

Lesson: Elon Musk's case highlights the power of self-reliance and resilience. The Lone Wolf is not afraid to stand alone and fight for their vision, even when no one else believes in it. Success is often built on the courage to forge ahead despite external doubt.

The Navy SEAL Operator: The Test of Independence

In the Navy SEALs, operators undergo rigorous training designed to test not just their physical endurance, but their mental toughness and independence. One of the toughest drills is the "isolation drill," where an operator is temporarily cut off from the rest of the team. The goal is to prove that the operator can think, fight, and execute without relying on the safety net of the team.

In these moments of isolation, SEALs learn to trust their instincts, make decisions under extreme pressure, and develop the mental toughness needed to perform in the most challenging conditions. The ability to function independently, even when isolated from the team, is a vital skill for any SEAL.

Lesson: The Navy SEALs exemplify the principle that leadership starts with self-reliance. True leaders can thrive when isolated, and their strength is tested when they must stand alone. This fosters independence, resilience, and clear thinking.

The Lone Athlete: Training in Silence

Some of the world's greatest athletes; boxers, marathon runners, and martial artists spend countless hours training in solitude. Their training is often done in silence, with no cheering crowds or applause. The hours spent running alone at dawn, working on the punching bag, or performing endless repetitions when no one is watching these are the moments where champions are made.

The lone athlete understands that personal growth comes from consistent effort in solitude, where focus and discipline can be cultivated without external distractions. It is in these quiet, solitary moments that they push themselves beyond their limits, honing the skills and mindset required to succeed.

Lesson: The lone athlete teaches us that greatness is often born in private discipline. Success is not about the spotlight, it is about what you do when no one is watching, what you build in the quiet moments of effort and self-reliance.

Abraham Lincoln: Solitude in Crisis

During the darkest days of the American Civil War, Abraham Lincoln often retreated into solitude. In these quiet moments, away from the pressure of political life, he found the clarity and strength he needed to make critical decisions. Lincoln is famously known for pacing the halls of the White House, often alone, thinking through the challenges the nation faced.

In these private moments, Lincoln sorted his thoughts, reflected on the future of the country, and disciplined his emotions before returning to address the nation. His ability to find calm and conviction in solitude allowed him to lead with a steady hand during one of the most tumultuous times in American history.

Lesson: Lincoln's leadership highlights the power of solitude in decision-making. True leaders find strength in silence, allowing themselves time to think deeply, reflect, and lead with clarity, especially during times of crisis.

The cases of Marcus Aurelius, Elon Musk, the Navy SEAL operator, and Abraham Lincoln all demonstrate the power of solitude and self-reliance in leadership. The Lone Wolf mentality is not about being isolated for the sake of isolation, but about developing the inner strength, resilience, and mental clarity needed to lead effectively. These leaders, through their willingness to stand alone and trust their inner vision, demonstrated that true leadership begins with self-reliance.

Whether it's in business, the military, athletics, or politics, the ability to function independently without the need for constant validation or external approval allows a leader to stay grounded, make clear decisions, and lead with unshakable confidence.

The Risks of Dependence

Dependence can seem comfortable, even tempting. In a world where social validation, group approval, and the safety of consensus are easily accessible, it's natural to lean on these comforts. Many people seek affirmation from the group and follow popular trends, believing it will guide them to success. But this comfort can be dangerous for a leader. Dependence on others for direction, approval, or motivation undermines the very foundation of leadership.

1. Dependence Weakens Decision-Making

When you rely on the approval of others or wait for consensus, your decision-making process becomes slow and diluted. Instead of acting with conviction, you begin to wait for others to speak up, adding unnecessary delays and uncertainties to every decision. A leader who depends on others to decide for them will often find themselves in a reactive role, rather than a proactive one.

This behavior creates a dangerous cycle where leadership becomes based on appeasing others rather than making sound, timely decisions. When you depend on others to approve of your choices, you risk compromising your leadership and turning it into a process of constant negotiation.

How It Works:

When faced with a decision, a leader should not be frozen by the need for external validation. The longer it takes to make a choice, the more opportunity there is for confusion to arise. Waiting for consensus invites uncertainty and stalls momentum. Dependence on approval results in leaders who hesitate at critical moments, undermining the speed of their actions and weakening their authority.

2. Dependence Erodes Discipline

A leader who is dependent on others' approval or feedback is also a leader who lacks inner discipline. Discipline is built from within. It's the ability to act, even when no one is watching. It's the strength to follow through on commitments, to stay focused on long-term goals, and to push through adversity without waiting for others to lead the way.

When a leader becomes accustomed to depending on others for validation or approval, it signals a lack of internal drive. The leader will only move when prompted or pushed by external forces. This constant external push diminishes the leader's own resilience and reduces the power of their actions.

How It Works:

Discipline isn't just about adhering to a schedule or following procedures. It's about taking ownership of your actions and decisions, even when it's inconvenient or unpopular. When leaders become accustomed to needing external validation, they lose the internal compass that drives self-reliance. Eventually, this can lead to burnout or a lack of progress, as the leader's energy is spent on seeking approval rather than pursuing their vision with independent conviction.

3. Dependence Blocks Growth

Growth thrives in environments where pressure challenges individuals to stretch their limits. When leaders are overly dependent on others, they become shielded from the kinds of pressures that force personal and professional growth. The discomfort that comes with making tough decisions, receiving criticism, or navigating failure is where growth occurs. But dependence on others to navigate these challenges prevents that growth from happening.

A dependent leader avoids stepping out of their comfort zone and resists the pressure that forges mastery. They shy away from risks or difficult situations, and this stunts their ability to grow into the full potential of their leadership.

How It Works:

By relying too heavily on group approval or external validation, leaders avoid confronting the difficult situations that lead to growth. The reality is, growth happens in the moments where you feel uncomfortable, where you're pushed beyond your current limits. When you remain in your comfort zone, you limit your capacity to learn and evolve.

In essence, dependency blocks access to the challenges and opportunities needed for leadership mastery. Leaders who shield themselves from discomfort also shield themselves from the valuable lessons and experiences that shape their leadership journey.

4. A Dependent Leader Collapses Under Criticism

When a leader relies too much on approval, they lack the internal strength needed to handle criticism. A dependent leader crumbles under feedback, whether it's negative or contrary to their vision. Instead of using criticism to improve and refine their leadership, they become defensive, avoiding tough conversations and steering clear of difficult calls.

A dependent leader may also resist necessary changes or adjustments, preferring to maintain the status quo because they fear the consequences of challenging others or upsetting the group. As a result, the team loses respect for the leader's authority and ability to make decisions.

How It Works:

When you depend on others for validation, you set yourself up to be vulnerable to criticism. Instead of seeing it as an opportunity to grow, you take it personally, leading to defensiveness, self-doubt, and ultimately, stagnation. A leader who cannot handle criticism will fail to navigate adversity effectively, diminishing their ability to lead with strength.

5. A Dependent Leader Avoids Difficult Calls

The hardest decisions are often the most crucial. Leaders are constantly faced with tough calls, from firing employees to making strategic shifts in the organization. A dependent leader avoids these decisions because they fear the reaction or the negative impact. They delay making calls, hoping that the situation will resolve itself or that someone else will step in.

This avoidance erodes the effectiveness of leadership. Leaders must be able to make difficult decisions, even when they know there will be pushback. A leader who avoids making tough calls creates confusion and instability, and the team will start to lose trust in their ability to lead.

How It Works:

Difficult decisions are part of leadership, and avoiding them only adds complexity to already challenging situations. A dependent leader may hesitate, second-guess themselves, or push tough decisions onto others. This can cause a lack of direction and accountability. Leaders who are independent and self-reliant take ownership of the decisions they make, even when they are hard or unpopular.

Dependence in leadership breeds insecurity, indecision, and stagnation. To be an effective leader, you must break free from the need for constant validation or approval from others. Leaders who are self-reliant are not deterred by criticism, nor are they bound by the expectations of others. They make decisions with clarity and confidence, guided by their vision and internal strength. The risks of dependence are clear: it weakens decision-making, erodes discipline, and blocks growth. Leadership built on independence, on the other hand, is unshakable. It is only by embracing self-reliance that you can lead with the strength, resilience, and clarity necessary to achieve your goals and inspire your team.

The path to true self-reliance doesn't happen overnight. It's about building discipline, mastering solitude, and overcoming the reliance on external validation. A lone wolf thrives in its solitude, not because it seeks isolation, but because it uses that time to strengthen its inner core. For a leader, this self-reliance is vital, it allows you to navigate through pressure with a clear mind and without needing the approval or validation of others.

1. Master Solitude

The first step in developing self-reliance is mastering solitude. Solitude isn't just about being physically alone it's about being comfortable in your own thoughts, facing the silence without distraction. Many people fear being alone with their thoughts, but true growth and clarity come from spending time in solitude.

How to Use It:

Spend at least one hour a day without phone, music, or conversation. This is time for you to walk, write, or simply think. The goal is to allow your mind to explore thoughts without the usual distractions of daily life. At first, this will be uncomfortable. Your mind will crave stimulation whether it's checking your phone or filling the silence with noise. However, over time, you'll find that this quiet time leads to greater clarity and deeper insights into yourself.

Why This Works:

Spending time in solitude strengthens your mind, allowing you to reconnect with your inner thoughts and intuition. It's in these moments of silence that your mind can process and problem-solve without external influences. This practice reconditions your brain, helping you build the mental resilience needed to lead decisively.

2. Break the Validation Addiction

In today's world, it's easy to become addicted to external validation. Likes, compliments, and approval from others can provide quick emotional rewards, but they also create an emotional dependency. True leadership, however, begins when you stop needing the approval of others and start relying on your internal validation.

How to Use It:

Start by noticing when you reach for external validation. Perhaps it's checking social media for likes, waiting for compliments, or looking for reassurance from others. Instead of giving in to these urges, practice replacing them with internal validation. For example, instead of seeking praise for your work, remind yourself: "I did the work. That is enough." Acknowledge your accomplishments, not based on others' reactions, but on your own standards.

Why This Works:

Breaking the validation addiction strengthens your confidence and leadership. You begin to trust yourself more and rely on your own judgment, rather than constantly seeking approval. This internal validation is vital for making decisions with clarity and conviction, regardless of outside opinions.

3. Build Self-Sufficiency

Self-reliance in small, everyday tasks builds the confidence needed to handle larger challenges. When you depend on others for too many things whether it's for cooking, managing your finances, or planning your fitness, you are subconsciously reinforcing the idea that you cannot rely on yourself. Building self-sufficiency in different areas of life trains your mind and body to act independently.

How to Use It:

Learn at least one skill you normally outsource. This could be something as simple as cooking a meal from scratch, managing your own budget, or planning a fitness routine. Starting with small tasks like these allows you to develop the mindset of self-reliance, empowering you to take control of your environment and decisions.

Why This Works:

Building self-sufficiency gives you the confidence to handle unexpected challenges. It forces you to rely on your own problem-solving skills and strengthens your ability to think and act without relying on others. When you can perform even the simplest tasks independently, you develop the mental fortitude needed for higher-level leadership.

4. Decision Drills

Leaders are constantly required to make decisions sometimes under extreme pressure. But making good decisions in high-stakes situations comes from practice. The more decisions you make, the sharper your decision-making ability becomes. By practicing smaller, less consequential decisions, you train your mind to be more decisive when the stakes are higher.

How to Use It:

Practice making quick decisions daily. Start with small choices: what to eat for lunch, which route to take, or what workout to do. The key is to make the decision quickly and stand by it. Don't second-guess yourself or overthink. The more you practice making quick decisions, the more confident you will become in your ability to make bigger, more impactful decisions when the pressure is on.

Why This Works:

This drill trains your brain to make decisions confidently, without hesitation. Over time, it builds the neural pathways necessary for decisive action, helping you become a leader who can make tough decisions quickly and effectively under pressure.

5. Controlled Discomfort

Growth doesn't happen in comfort. It happens when we challenge ourselves, step outside our comfort zone, and face discomfort head-on. The lone wolf embraces discomfort, knowing that this is where the greatest growth lies. Whether it's physical discomfort or mental discomfort, training yourself to endure and thrive in these moments builds resilience.

How to Use It:

Expose yourself to discomfort regularly. This could be through physical challenges like cold showers, solo travel, or endurance workouts. You could also practice discomfort in social settings like speaking up in a meeting when your opinion is unpopular. The goal is to make discomfort a regular part of your routine, so your mind and body learn to operate under pressure.

Why This Works:

Controlled discomfort builds mental toughness and resilience. The more you put yourself in uncomfortable situations, the more you train your nervous system to stay calm and focused when it matters most. As a leader, the ability to stay composed under pressure is one of your most powerful tools.

Science Expansion – Solitude & the Brain

Solitude, when practiced intentionally, has profound effects on the brain, especially in enhancing creativity, problem-solving, and long-term vision. In today's world, we are constantly bombarded by distractions; constant notifications, social media updates, and the never-ending noise of modern life. Yet, when we take time to step away from these external stimuli, our brain enters a state that promotes deeper thinking and stronger cognitive connections.

How Solitude Strengthens the Brain:

1. The Default Mode Network:

The brain's Default Mode Network (DMN) is a system associated with creativity, problem-solving, and introspection. Solitude allows the DMN to activate, as the absence of external distractions gives our brain the space it needs to wander and connect ideas more fluidly. Many breakthroughs and creative insights often occur in moments of solitude, when we're free from the constant noise of daily life. These moments allow our brain to engage in abstract thinking, processing ideas in ways we might miss when constantly multitasking or overstimulated.

2. Neuroplasticity and Cognitive Flexibility:

Neuroplasticity refers to the brain's ability to reorganize itself by forming new neural connections throughout life. Solitude can stimulate neuroplasticity by offering the brain the chance to form these new connections without the clutter of external input. When you engage in deep thinking or reflection during solitary moments, your brain can rewire itself to solve problems more efficiently and develop a deeper understanding of complex ideas.

3. Dopamine and Reward Systems:

In a world that constantly feeds us quick rewards such as likes on social media or instant feedback, our brains become accustomed to seeking constant novelty and external validation. This dependence on instant gratification increases dopamine levels in our brain. However, solitude has the opposite effect. It allows our dopamine levels to rebalance, teaching the brain to find satisfaction in patience, deep thought, and long-term rewards rather than fleeting moments of approval. This rewiring of the brain helps foster the ability to focus, persevere, and stay grounded in the pursuit of long-term goals.

4. Cortisol Reduction – Stress Resilience:

The hormone cortisol, often associated with stress, is typically elevated when we are overwhelmed or anxious. However, regular periods of solitude have been shown to lower cortisol levels, which helps regulate emotional balance. Solitude allows the brain and body to reset and recover from stress, improving resilience in the face of pressure. As a result, those who spend time in solitude can remain calmer under stress, maintaining clarity and focus when it's needed most. For the lone wolf, this means developing a calm, unshakable presence even in the most chaotic circumstances.

Why This Matters for Leadership?

The connection between solitude and the brain is crucial for leadership. Leaders who embrace solitude are not only able to think more clearly and creatively, but they also build the mental resilience needed to lead in high-pressure situations. By training the brain through intentional solitude, you learn to remain calm, focused, and decisive—even when external forces are pushing you in every direction.

From Solitude to Strength

The lone wolf is not a permanent exile, it is a training ground. Without independence, leadership collapses under pressure. With independence, leadership multiplies in strength. The period of standing alone sharpens instincts, disciplines emotion, and builds credibility. When the wolf rejoins the pack, he brings back not just loyalty, but clarity and resilience that cannot be shaken. The leader who has learned to endure without constant validation becomes unmovable when the crowd returns. This is the true advantage of the lone wolf: strength born in silence, carried back into leadership with unshakable presence.

Closing: The Wolf Becomes the Leader

The lone wolf stage is not permanent exile; it is essential training. A wolf who never learns independence will remain vulnerable, unable to thrive under pressure. However, the wolf who builds strength in solitude becomes unshakable when it rejoins the pack.

Leadership demands this first test. Before commanding others, you must prove you can command yourself. Before asking for loyalty, you must show that you can walk the path alone. The true power of leadership lies in your ability to stand firm without external validation, maintaining your direction regardless of the opinions of others.

The Lone Wolf Advantage is not about abandoning the group. It's about cultivating such inner strength that when you return to lead, no storm, no criticism, and no abandonment can destabilize you. By mastering solitude, you fortify yourself mentally, emotionally, and psychologically.

When the wolf returns to the pack after solitude, it is no longer needy but strong. It leads not with the validation of the crowd, but with a clarity and resilience forged in isolation. The leader who has learned to endure without external reinforcement brings an unshakable presence to the team. This strength, born in silence, will guide others through uncertainty and challenge, becoming the anchor in turbulent times.

Daily Routine:

- **Morning:** Begin each day with 10 minutes of silence before using your phone or any media. This simple act conditions your mind to seek clarity before being bombarded with external distractions.
- **Midday:** Practice one independence drill. Make a small decision quickly — such as choosing your lunch, your work task, or the route you'll take home — without seeking input. Follow through confidently.
- **Evening:** Journal in your Lone Wolf Log. Reflect on one choice you made that day without seeking approval. Consider how it felt to act independently, without relying on others' opinions.

Weekly Challenge:

Week 1: Digital Solitude

- **Task:** Spend one hour offline each day.
- **Goal:** Reflect on the distractions you crave most.
- **Why It Works:** This helps you recognize and control your impulses for constant connection, giving your mind space to focus and regain clarity.

Week 2: Independent Action

- **Task:** Complete a project alone from start to finish.
- **Goal:** No outsourcing, no help.

- **Why It Works:** This drill builds your self-reliance and ability to execute on your own, strengthening your confidence and independence in real-world tasks.

Week 3: Public Independence

- **Task:** Share an unpopular but principled opinion in conversation.
- **Goal:** Stand by it calmly, regardless of how others respond.
- **Why It Works**: Practicing public independence allows you to test your ability to stand firm in your beliefs without external validation, reinforcing inner strength.

Week 4: Discomfort Challenge

- **Task:** Do one activity solo that you'd normally only attempt in a group (e.g., dining out, training, public speaking practice).
- **Goal:** Journal the resistance and growth you experience.
- **Why It Works:** This challenge strengthens your ability to function alone, increasing your comfort with discomfort and fostering mental resilience.

Outcome:

By the end of four weeks, you will no longer merely tolerate solitude — you'll begin to value it as a source of personal strength. You'll have trained your mind to operate independently, with a foundation of clarity, confidence, and inner resilience.

Reflection Prompts

1. When was the last time I chose solitude deliberately instead of avoiding it?

Reflect on the last time you embraced solitude instead of running from it. What were the feelings and insights that came from choosing isolation for growth or clarity?

2. Which areas of my life still depend too heavily on approval from others?

Pinpoint specific instances where you seek validation in your personal or professional life. What steps can you take to reduce this dependence and rely more on your internal judgment?

3. How might I train myself to function at full capacity even when support is absent?

Consider situations where you lack support or approval. How can you condition yourself to act independently, even when the external environment isn't providing the usual reassurance?

4. If I had to carry forward with only my inner resources for 30 days, what habits would sustain me?

Imagine a scenario where you're completely on your own, with no external influence or validation. What practices or routines can you develop that will keep you focused, grounded, and productive without relying on others?

CHAPTER
8

Battling the Desires of the Flesh: Discipline Over Impulse

Leadership requires strength of character, and that strength is tested most fiercely not by external enemies, but by the inner desires that pull us in different directions. These desires; comfort, lust, greed, laziness, and indulgence have the potential to derail the strongest leaders, often more effectively than any external threat.

Leaders who fail to conquer their inner appetites do not simply falter; they can be brought to ruin. The battle of the flesh is universal and timeless. If you look closely at the fall of great empires or the downfall of dynasties, you'll see a pattern: the leaders who lost their discipline and gave into indulgence are often the ones who ignited their own decline. It is not always an external enemy that destroys, but the internal surrender to fleeting pleasures and unchecked desires.

This is a battle every individual face, not just those in power. It's easy to point to external forces as the cause of failure — but the truth is that real strength lies in resisting the pull of these immediate desires. To be truly powerful, you must master the very body and impulses that seem to command your every move.

Mastering the flesh is not about complete denial it's about control. True mastery comes from owning your body and desires rather than being controlled by them. Discipline is the path to freedom. When you can command your impulses, you unlock the ability to achieve great things. Conversely, when those desires rule you, you are enslaved by them.

Why Discipline Over Impulse is the Core of Leadership

In leadership, the ability to control your impulses and desires is paramount. Leaders who lack self-discipline fail to lead themselves, and thus, they cannot lead others effectively. The strongest leaders are not the ones who simply win battles against external forces; they are the ones who win the battle against themselves.

This battle is not a one-time effort, nor is it a path that ends. It is ongoing, a daily test of your willpower and your ability to remain focused on long-term goals, despite the allure of immediate gratification.

When you understand that discipline over impulse is the ultimate differentiator between success and failure, you become unstoppable. The greatest leaders in history were not those who had everything — they were the ones who understood that true power comes from within, from the ability to reign over desires and focus on the higher goal.

The Science of Impulse and Craving

The desire for immediate gratification is deeply wired into our brains. It's not just a matter of willpower it's a biological force that governs much of our behavior. From junk food to social media, we're constantly exposed to stimuli that trigger powerful chemical reactions in our brain, reinforcing the cycle of impulse and pleasure.

Cravings are not just moments of weakness; they are powerful biochemical signals that originate deep within your brain. Understanding the biology behind cravings can give you greater control over them and enhance your ability to exercise discipline in the face of temptation. Every craving you feel is the result of chemical reactions that are hardwired into your brain and body. However, by recognizing these signals, you can train yourself to make better decisions and take back control.

1. Dopamine Spikes: The False Reward System

Dopamine, the brain's "feel-good" chemical, plays a central role in our desires and addictions. It's responsible for the pleasure we feel when we indulge in activities like eating junk food, watching pornography, drinking alcohol, or mindlessly scrolling through social media. These activities flood the brain with dopamine, providing a short burst of satisfaction.

However, this quick fix is deceptive. It teaches the brain to crave immediate pleasure rather than the deeper, more satisfying rewards that come from effort and discipline. When we engage in these instant-gratification behaviors, we reinforce the habit of seeking pleasure without working for it, which is why breaking the cycle becomes so challenging. Over time, these rewards lose their power to satisfy, and we are left chasing the next hit of dopamine, caught in a cycle of addiction to easy pleasure.

2. The Limbic System: Your Primal Brain

The limbic system, often referred to as the "primal brain," is the area responsible for survival instincts, reproduction, and basic drives for comfort and safety. This system is powerful, and when unchecked, it can override the more rational part of your brain; the prefrontal cortex.

The prefrontal cortex is the area of the brain responsible for higher-order thinking, planning, and self-control. In moments of impulse, however, the primal limbic system tends to take control, compelling you to prioritize short-term comfort over long-term goals. Without discipline, this primal system can dominate, pushing you toward immediate gratification at the expense of your future well-being.

3. Cortisol and Cravings: The Stress-Desire Connection

Stress is one of the biggest amplifiers of cravings. When you experience emotional or physical stress, your body releases cortisol, a hormone that prepares you to handle pressure. However, cortisol also increases the likelihood of seeking comfort through food, alcohol, or distractions, as your body seeks relief from stress-induced tension.

When you lack emotional control, cortisol levels rise, leading you to chase quick pleasures — like comfort food or binge-watching shows — as a way to temporarily soothe your nervous system. This cycle of stress and indulgence creates a feedback loop that reinforces unhealthy habits and weakens your self-control.

4. Neuroplasticity: The Path to Habitual Discipline

The good news is that you can rewire your brain. Neuroplasticity, the brain's ability to form and reorganize synaptic connections, allows you to create new habits through consistent effort. Every time you resist temptation, your brain carves a new neural pathway, reinforcing the practice of discipline over impulse.

In other words, every small victory over temptation strengthens your ability to make better decisions in the future. The more you practice resisting your immediate desires, the easier it becomes to make disciplined choices. Eventually, what once required effort becomes second nature. Discipline becomes a habit i.e a mental muscle that you continue to build, not a temporary effort.

Hunger and Hormones

Our cravings are deeply intertwined with hunger, which is regulated by two important hormones: ghrelin and leptin.

Ghrelin: The Hunger Signal

Ghrelin, often referred to as the "hunger hormone," spikes before meals, signaling to your body that it's time to eat. It triggers feelings of hunger, motivating you to seek food. However, many of the cravings we experience are not caused by true physical hunger but by false alarms driven by stress or routine. For example, when you're stressed or bored, your body might crave comfort foods even though you're not actually hungry.

Discipline involves recognizing the surge of ghrelin and resisting the impulse to eat when it isn't truly necessary. By waiting and allowing your body to adjust, you train yourself to resist unnecessary indulgence, thereby restoring your control over your eating habits.

Leptin: The Fullness Signal

Leptin is the hormone responsible for signaling fullness to the brain, telling you when to stop eating. When leptin is functioning properly, it helps regulate your appetite and keeps you from overeating. Unfortunately, in a world full of constant temptation, leptin's signals can be overridden by excessive eating or emotional stress. The more you engage in dopamine-driven snacking, the less responsive your leptin becomes, making it harder to know when you're actually full.

Practicing self-discipline by engaging in fasting or controlled eating patterns can help reset your leptin system. This process restores natural hunger cycles, allowing your body to recognize when it truly needs food and when it doesn't.

The Connection Between Ghrelin and Leptin

Together, ghrelin and leptin illustrate a crucial principle: hunger and cravings are signals, not commands. The disciplined individual learns to read these signals but doesn't necessarily act on them. By training yourself to identify true hunger versus emotional cravings, you build the inner strength needed to make deliberate, mindful choices.

Discipline in Relationships

Discipline is often thought of in terms of self-control over food, sleep, or physical indulgence. However, the desires of the flesh extend far beyond these simple pleasures. In fact, the most destructive impulses we face often show up in our relationships, lust, envy, and unchecked ego. These forces, if left unchecked, can erode the foundation of trust, respect, and authority that a leader relies upon to maintain influence. A leader who succumbs to these emotional urges' risks losing credibility, regardless of their skill, intelligence, or strategic vision.

At its core, discipline in relationships is about control over impulses that threaten the integrity of our connections with others. These desires whether they are the allure of power, the temptation to indulge in pride, or the grip of lust have the potential to undermine the trust and respect others place in us. Leaders are not immune to these challenges, and the ability to control them is often what distinguishes great leaders from those who fall short.

The Bottom Line: Leaders who master their desires in relationships unlock the true power of influence. When a leader is not ruled by ego, lust, or envy, their relationships become stronger, more authentic, and more resilient. This is the discipline that separates lasting, impactful leadership from short-lived success. Leadership is not about exerting control over others but about demonstrating the control you have over yourself. It's about leading with integrity and purpose, where every interaction is guided by principles and mutual respect, not fleeting emotions or selfish desires.

Case Studies in Mastery Over Impulse

Case 1: The Athlete's Resilience: Discipline Beyond Talent

Consider a professional athlete who's known not just for his incredible skill but also for his unwavering commitment to discipline. He's well-known for making tough choices, such as rejecting temptations for foods and habits that could shorten his career. This self-discipline enabled him to extend his career, perform at elite levels, and maintain peak physical condition despite external pressures.

Lesson: The essence of leadership is consistent discipline, especially when it comes to managing temptations and cravings. Leaders who avoid indulgence, whether it's food, comfort, or distractions, create more space for their talents and ideas to flourish. Discipline leads to sustained success.

Case 2: Everyday Leaders: Quiet Victories in Solitude

In everyday life, there are leaders who may not hold grand titles but who exhibit the quiet strength of the lone wolf. Parents, entrepreneurs, and workers who wake up early, dedicate time for personal growth, and sacrifice comfort to work towards their goals, these individuals are the unseen leaders who show up every day and make decisions based on long-term vision rather than immediate pleasure.

Lesson: Leadership is not only shown in grand gestures but in daily choices. It's the everyday decisions to forgo comfort and instant pleasure that form the backbone of true leadership.

Case 3: David Goggins: Overcoming the Body's Weakness

David Goggins, who transformed from an overweight, struggling individual into a Navy SEAL and ultramarathon runner, exemplifies the power of discipline over physical and mental weakness. He rejected comfort and pushed through unimaginable pain, embodying the principle that the body's desires can be overcome through relentless discipline.

Lesson: Relentless discipline in the face of adversity allows leaders to push past personal limitations. Goggins' story shows how mastery over the body translates into unparalleled mental and leadership strength.

Case 4: Steve Jobs: Discipline in Minimalism

Steve Jobs' discipline extended beyond his work at Apple. He practiced minimalism, fasting, and simplifying his life to reduce distractions. His focus on self-discipline and simplicity helped him maintain a sharp vision and drive creativity, ultimately leading to Apple's success.

Lesson: Simplicity and discipline are at the heart of innovation. Jobs' story reminds us that to create something truly groundbreaking, we must strip away the unnecessary and focus on what truly matters.

Case 5: The Spartans: Training in Austerity

From childhood, Spartan soldiers were trained to reject comfort and pleasure, embracing hardship and austerity. This rigorous training-built soldiers who could endure battle without flinching. Their power wasn't in their ability to indulge; it was in their ability to endure.

Lesson: True strength is forged in discipline, especially in moments of discomfort. The Spartans' ability to resist temptation and discomfort made them some of the most formidable warriors in history.

Training the Will Against the Flesh

This section is dedicated to building discipline by teaching you how to control your impulses, delay gratification, and turn cravings into opportunities for growth. True strength comes not from avoiding discomfort but from choosing to endure and grow through it.

1. Delay Gratification

The first step in mastering your impulses is learning to delay gratification. In our fast-paced world, we are constantly bombarded with instant rewards. Whether it's a quick sugar fix, social media scrolling, or a momentary indulgence, the temptation to satisfy desires immediately is ever-present. However, true leaders know that instant gratification undermines long-term success.

How to Use It:

- Start by saying "not now" to cravings. The next time you feel the urge to indulge in a comfort or distraction, tell yourself to wait for 15 minutes. During this time, engage in something productive or simply breathe through the craving. The more you practice this delay, the more you train your brain to resist impulsive behavior.

Why This Works:

- By delaying gratification, you build the muscle of patience and self-control. Over time, you'll notice that cravings lose their power. What initially seemed like an urgent need will become just a passing thought, and you will feel more in control of your actions and choices.

2. Physical Conditioning: Daily Reminders of Discipline

Physical conditioning is an excellent way to train your willpower and remind yourself of your ability to command your body. Every time you push yourself in a workout, you reinforce the belief that you control your body, not the other way around.

How to Use It:

- View each workout not just as a means of health but as a moment of discipline training. Every rep, every run, is an act of rebellion against laziness. Push yourself to the limits of discomfort and notice how your mind responds to the resistance. This will help you stay grounded and resilient when other, more tempting, desires arise in daily life.

Why This Works:

- Physical conditioning taps directly into your mental fortitude. It's a constant reminder that you control what happens in your body, not your impulses. Every moment of discomfort you endure strengthens your ability to resist indulgence in other areas of life.

3. Cold Exposure & Fasting: Voluntary Discomfort

One of the most effective ways to recondition your nervous system and build resilience is to expose yourself to voluntary discomfort. Cold showers and fasting are two of the most powerful methods for training the body and mind to thrive outside of comfort zones.

How to Use It:

- Cold Showers: Start incorporating cold showers into your daily routine. Begin with a 30-second cold shower at the end of your regular shower and gradually increase the duration.

- Fasting: Implement intermittent fasting or try a 24-hour food fast once a week. The purpose of fasting is not only physical purification but mental fortitude showing yourself that you can endure discomfort without the immediate reward of food.

Why This Works:

Both cold exposure and fasting disrupt the body's craving for comfort and indulgence. They teach the body to regulate its responses to stress and discomfort, which will transfer to other areas of your life. When you can resist the urge to find comfort in food or warmth, you reinforce your mental resilience.

4. Eliminate Triggers

Another critical part of mastering your impulses is identifying and removing triggers that lead to indulgence. We often expose ourselves to situations where cravings are easily satisfied, making the fight for control that much harder. By proactively eliminating these triggers, you make discipline a natural choice.

How to Use It:

- Take inventory of the triggers in your environment. Is there a particular time of day when you're most likely to give into cravings? Is there a place you visit that leads to bad habits? Identify these triggers and remove them or replace them with healthier alternatives.

Why This Works:

- The fewer temptations you face, the easier it is to maintain control. Discipline becomes less about willpower and more about creating an environment that supports your growth. By eliminating temptation, you reduce the number of decisions you have to make, making it easier to stay on track.

5. Replace, Don't Just Resist

Merely resisting cravings can feel like a constant battle. Instead, focus on replacing unhealthy habits with productive alternatives. This creates a shift in your mindset, allowing you to view the craving as an opportunity to strengthen a new, more positive habit.

How to Use It:

When a craving arises, rather than simply saying "no," redirect the energy into something productive. For instance:

- Hunger → Exercise: If you feel a craving for junk food, go for a short walk or do a quick workout instead.
- Boredom → Reading: When you feel the urge to scroll mindlessly, pick up a book or engage in a hobby.
- Lust → Creativity: Redirect sexual energy into creative pursuits, such as writing or painting.

Why This Works:

- By replacing indulgence with productive alternatives, you turn your cravings into opportunities for personal growth. This not only makes the process of resisting easier but also strengthens positive habits that support your long-term vision.

Weekly Mission – Flesh Discipline

The weekly mission focuses on gradually building discipline in real-life scenarios. By engaging in practical challenges, you will learn to combat desires and impulses, ultimately making discipline a more natural part of your lifestyle.

- Week 1: Track your daily cravings and delay their response by 10 minutes. Focus on observing and acknowledging your impulses without immediately satisfying them.
- Week 2: Add one voluntary discomfort activity to your week, such as a cold shower, fasting, or waking up earlier than usual. Use this discomfort as an opportunity to build mental strength.
- Week 3: Choose one indulgence to eliminate completely whether it's junk food, alcohol, or endless social media scrolling. Notice how your mind and body respond.
- Week 4: Replace one major craving with a constructive habit. Redirect your impulse into a productive activity such as exercise, deep work, or learning.

By the end of these four weeks, you'll start to see the power of delayed gratification and the strength that comes from resisting impulse. Most impulses, when not acted on, will naturally dissipate.

Reflection Prompts

What desire has the most power over me?

Take a moment to reflect on the desires or cravings that consistently pull you away from your goals. Is it comfort, food, social validation, or something else? Identify the specific cravings that have the greatest impact on your leadership and discipline. Understanding this is the first step to reclaiming control.

Do I control my body, or does my body control me?

Leadership starts with self-mastery. Consider whether you've allowed your body's urges to dictate your actions, from indulgence in comfort food to the craving for distraction. Do you have the willpower to make conscious choices or are you acting based on impulses?

Which cravings sabotage my leadership or clarity?

Reflect on how specific cravings, whether they be for instant pleasure, distractions, or comfort, have hindered your ability to lead with clarity. When you're caught in the grip of indulgence, what are you sacrificing in terms of focus, decision-making, and leadership?

If I removed one indulgence for 30 days, how would my life change?

Think about the habits or indulgences you rely on—perhaps alcohol, junk food, or mindless scrolling. What would happen if you eliminated just one of these for a month? How would it affect your physical, mental, and emotional well-being? What positive changes might you see in your leadership and clarity?

Picture two versions of yourself:

- **Version 1:** The one who is enslaved by cravings. This version reacts impulsively to every desire taking the easy route, seeking comfort, and avoiding discomfort. Leadership is muddled by lack of clarity, and trust is weak, as people see you constantly swayed by outside influences.
- **Version 2:** The disciplined, calm, and free version of yourself. This version stands firm against cravings, makes decisions with purpose, and leads with clarity. Instead of reacting, you pause, reflect, and act with integrity. People trust you because they see your consistency and strength.

Now, reflect on which version earns trust, builds respect, and fulfills purpose. Each choice you make today shapes which version of you becomes real tomorrow. Will you continue to be reactive to cravings, or will you cultivate discipline and self-mastery to build a stronger, more effective leader?

Closing: Discipline as Freedom

The desires of the flesh promise freedom, but they ultimately deliver slavery. Every craving obeyed tightens the chains of dependency, while each craving resisted sharpens the sword of discipline. The path to true freedom isn't about indulging every desire; it's about mastering them.

Leaders who control their impulses stand apart. They are rare but enduring. Their teams, families, and communities trust them because they are not swayed by momentary appetites or fleeting urges. These leaders operate with a clear purpose, and their ability to make decisions free from the control of cravings earns them respect and loyalty. They lead by example, showing that true power lies not in following the flesh, but in overcoming it.

Discipline over the flesh is not punishment it is the highest form of freedom. It is the power to act with purpose and intention, not to react impulsively to every desire. This discipline frees the mind, redirects energy toward higher goals, and strengthens the resolve needed to guide others.

Final Reinforcement

Mastering the desires of the flesh goes beyond simply resisting temptation; it unlocks a higher level of leadership. When the body no longer dictates the mind, energy is no longer wasted on fleeting pleasures. Instead, it's redirected into what truly matters—vision, clarity, and action.

Each indulgence resisted sharpens discipline. Each impulse conquered strengthens authority. Leaders who win the private war against cravings are able to exude a steady, unwavering presence in the public eye. People instinctively trust them because they sense that steadiness.

Victory over the flesh becomes the foundation for success in all other areas of life. Without it, even the most talented and gifted leader will eventually collapse under their own weaknesses. It is not just about resisting temptation; it is about building the inner strength required to lead with clarity, consistency, and purpose.

CHAPTER
9

Nutrition for the Mind and Body: Fueling Discipline and Clarity.

Why Nutrition Matters for Leadership

Leadership is fought on multiple fronts, but the most consistent battles are fought within the self. You cannot think, act, or lead like a warrior if you are fueling your body with excess, indulgence, or poor choices. Nutrition is not simply about filling the stomach it is the foundation of clarity, focus, and resilience. The body is the battlefield where discipline is either reinforced or undermined. Every choice you make in what you consume has a direct impact on your ability to act decisively and think clearly.

History is full of examples of leaders undone by indulgence. Overeating, chronic alcohol use, and neglect of physical health have eroded careers, sapped mental sharpness, and clouded judgment. On the other hand, leaders who mastered their diet-maintained energy, mental clarity, and endurance long after their peers faltered. Their bodies became tools of discipline rather than vessels of distraction.

Nutrition is not merely a measure to prevent disease, it is a strategy to sharpen the mind, strengthen willpower, and ensure your body responds to the commands of the mind. Every meal is an opportunity: to reinforce self-control, optimize performance, and fortify your capacity to act with intention in every high-stakes moment.

The Science of Food and Focus

To understand why nutrition matters for leadership, it's essential to grasp the science behind how food directly affects your mental clarity, focus, and decision-making. The brain is incredibly energy-intensive and requires a consistent supply of nutrients to function optimally. But what you feed it can either enhance your abilities or hinder them.

Glucose and Focus: The brain runs primarily on glucose, a form of sugar derived from the food we consume. However, when blood sugar spikes and crashes often due to processed sugars or fast carbs your focus wavers, and your decision-making ability declines. Stable blood sugar levels help maintain mental clarity and allow for more rational, disciplined thinking. Therefore, choosing foods that provide sustained energy, such as whole grains and lean proteins, is essential for steady leadership.

Omega-3 Fatty Acids: Essential fatty acids, like omega-3s found in fish, walnuts, and flaxseeds, are crucial for memory, mood regulation, and brain function. These healthy fats are involved in the formation of neurotransmitters, which are vital for clear communication within the brain. By incorporating these into your diet, you fuel not just your body, but your brain's ability to perform under pressure.

Micronutrients: Magnesium, zinc, and B vitamins play key roles in energy production, stress reduction, and overall mental wellness. These nutrients help regulate mood and ensure that your body and mind can handle the demands of leadership without succumbing to fatigue or anxiety.

Inflammation and Mood: Chronic inflammation, which is often exacerbated by processed food, can significantly impact mood, leading to irritability and stress. By avoiding inflammatory foods, you reduce the risk of mood swings, allowing you to maintain calm and focus, even during high-pressure situations.

Gut-Brain Axis: The gut is often called the "second brain" because it plays a significant role in our mental well-being. Approximately 90% of serotonin, the "feel-good" neurotransmitter, is produced in the gut. What you eat directly impacts this serotonin production, which in turn affects your ability to stay calm, focused, and clear-headed under pressure. Therefore, what you choose to consume matters not only for your body but for your emotional and cognitive stability.

Training Your Nutritional Discipline

Mastering discipline over your diet requires consistent practice and self-awareness. Nutrition isn't about denying yourself pleasure; it's about making deliberate choices that support your body and mind. By training your nutritional discipline, you not only build your body's resilience but also sharpen your leadership.

Food Awareness

Start by tracking everything you eat for a week. This helps identify patterns, such as sugar cravings, alcohol consumption, or reliance on processed foods. Awareness is the first step toward control. Once you've tracked your intake, you can see where your nutrition is supporting your goals and where it's hindering them.

Simplify the Plate

Build meals around three key elements: protein, vegetables, and healthy fats. Keep it simple and consistent. Complex meals with too many ingredients often lead to decision fatigue, and in leadership, simplicity is a key to focus. Stick to a routine that supports your energy and cognitive performance.

Intermittent Fasting

Intermittent fasting isn't just about limiting food intake; it's about training your body to delay gratification. By fasting for 14–16 hours a day, you help reset your body's metabolic processes and boost your mental clarity. This practice teaches patience and reinforces discipline both vital qualities for a leader. Begin by fasting for 12 hours and gradually extend it.

Hydration Discipline

Dehydration reduces cognitive function, making it harder to stay focused and make sound decisions. Start your day with water, adding electrolytes if needed. This simple habit helps keep your mind sharp. Avoid relying on caffeine or sugary drinks to fuel your day; instead, choose hydration as your first source of energy.

Strategic Indulgence

Discipline doesn't mean you can never indulge. It means controlling when and how you indulge. Plan your indulgences in advance whether it's a meal or a break so they don't derail your overall goals. Discipline lies not in avoidance, but in control and timing.

Leadership Connection

Nutrition is the foundation of discipline. A leader who indulges in excess food or alcohol soon demonstrates the same lack of control in other areas money, speech, or decisions. Mastering your appetite builds trust, as others recognize your steadiness. Food is not just fuel it is the daily test of leadership."

Historical Contrast – Leaders Undone by Indulgence

History shows that poor nutrition and indulgence can undermine even the most capable leaders. Leaders who succumbed to excessive eating, rich foods, or constant indulgence often lost mental clarity and physical stamina at critical moments. Their vulnerability was not only strategic but physiological; fatigue, stress, and impaired focus created cracks in judgment and resilience.

In contrast, disciplined leaders approached food intentionally, treating it as fuel rather than mere pleasure. Consistent, mindful eating habits preserved energy, sharpened cognitive performance, and sustained endurance through demanding situations. These leaders-maintained focus under pressure, made clearer decisions, and avoided the pitfalls of impulsive cravings.

The lesson is timeless: leadership thrives when the body supports the mind. Discipline at the table is discipline in action. By controlling indulgence and prioritizing nutrition, leaders equip themselves with the stamina, focus, and resilience needed to meet challenges decisively. Mastery over the flesh translates directly into clarity, authority, and the ability to lead with consistency when it matters most.

Nutrition as Leadership Armor

Food is never just food. Each choice at the table is a rehearsal for the choices you will make in battle, business, and family life. When you build the discipline to nourish your body with intention, you are training the muscles of restraint and foresight needed for leadership.

Skipping junk food today is practice for avoiding shortcuts tomorrow. Choosing hydration over alcohol is training for clarity over confusion when the stakes are high.

Your family and your followers absorb your habits. A leader who eats with discipline models control, vision, and respect for the vessel he has been given. A leader who indulges recklessly teaches weakness and compromise. Nutrition ripples outward, shaping not just your own energy but the standards of those who look to you for guidance.

When crises strike, the leader who has built his body into armor will stand steady. His decisions will not be clouded by fatigue or dulled by indulgence. Nutrition is not a side detail; it is central to the making of a warrior-leader.

Case Studies – Discipline in Nutrition

Discipline in nutrition is a cornerstone of both physical resilience and mental clarity. Across history and modern practice, leaders and high performers have demonstrated that control over the body translates directly into control over decisions, focus, and endurance.

Case 1: The Spartan Approach – Ancient warriors thrived on simplicity: black broth, barley, and dried fruits. Their austere diet kept soldiers lean, resilient, and prepared for prolonged campaigns. These basic meals trained both body and mind, proving that restraint and consistency are as essential as skill or strength. Simplicity on the plate translated into clarity in decision-making and endurance under pressure.

Case 2: Modern Military Training – Elite units follow precise fueling plans designed for sustained energy, hydration, and mental alertness rather than luxury. Meals composed of lean proteins, complex carbohydrates, and electrolytes enable long operations, showing that structured nutrition strengthens discipline, readiness, and resilience.

Case 3: High-Performing Leaders and Athletes – Many high achievers today treat nutrition as a strategic tool. Intermittent fasting, protein-focused meals, and minimizing processed foods sharpen focus, sustain energy, and reinforce daily discipline. Nutrition becomes a lever for performance, demonstrating that control over the body strengthens control over choices and actions.

Practical Framework – Daily Warrior Eating

Below is a simple yet effective eating structure to build your daily routine around, ensuring your body works as efficiently as your mind.

Morning:

- Start the day with hydration to kickstart your metabolism. A glass of water with electrolytes or lemon sets the tone for clarity and energy. If you're practicing intermittent fasting, delay eating until midday. If you're eating, keep it light—focus on protein and healthy fats (e.g., eggs, avocado, or nuts). This stabilizes your blood sugar and primes your body and mind for focus.

Midday:

- Anchor your day with a balanced meal: lean protein (chicken, fish, tofu), vegetables (spinach, broccoli, kale), and slow-digesting carbs (sweet potatoes, quinoa). This meal fuels your productivity, keeping you energized and preventing the mid-day crash that so many experiences. It's about giving your body what it needs to maintain focus, not just to fill you up.

Evening:

- Eat lighter in the evening to promote recovery. Focus on controlled portions of protein (fish, lean meat), leafy greens (kale, spinach), and healthy fats (olive oil, nuts). This helps your body repair without burdening your digestive system before sleep, allowing for deeper rest.

Supplements:

To enhance performance and well-being, consider adding essential supplements:

- Omega-3s for improved brain function and reduced inflammation.
- Magnesium for muscle recovery and relaxation.
- Vitamin D for immune function, energy, and mood.
- Electrolytes for sustained focus and hydration.

Keep your choices simple to avoid decision fatigue. Each supplement should have a clear, specific purpose.

30-Day Nutrition Reset

Resetting your nutrition is about building habits, not depriving yourself. This 30-day program helps you develop sustainable, disciplined eating routines that serve both your body and your leadership role.

Week 1: Track Everything

- Begin by tracking everything you eat for a week. This helps you become aware of any unhealthy patterns or habits, such as excessive sugar or alcohol consumption. Remove soda, alcohol, and excessive sugar from your diet during this first week. The goal is to begin building awareness and eliminating the most disruptive foods.

Week 2: Protein-Based Meals

- Shift to protein-based meals with a focus on vegetables. Cut out processed foods, and instead, focus on whole, nutrient-dense meals. Your body will begin to adjust to higher-quality fuel, improving energy levels and focus. Simplicity is key—don't overcomplicate your meals.

Week 3: Intermittent Fasting

- Introduce intermittent fasting. Start with a 12-hour fasting window, from, for example, 7 PM to 7 AM. Gradually extend it to 16 hours. Use the extra time for mental clarity, exercise, or productivity. Track how fasting affects your clarity, mental discipline, and energy. It's not just about delaying food—it's about training your body to operate with greater patience and focus.

Week 4: Strategic Indulgence

- By now, you've built new eating habits. It's time to plan indulgences, rather than reacting impulsively. Once a week, allow yourself a controlled indulgence—whether it's a dessert, a favorite snack, or a meal outside your usual routine. Journal how you feel after your indulgence to reflect on whether it was worth the temporary pleasure. Focus on awareness rather than guilt.

By the end of these 30 days, food will no longer be a source of excess or indulgence. It will be fuel—purposeful and aligned with your leadership goals.

Reflection Prompts

Reflection is key to understanding how your eating habits align with your leadership goals. Take the time to honestly assess how your diet influences your ability to lead with clarity, discipline, and focus.

Do I eat for strength or comfort?

- Reflect on your relationship with food. Are your choices driven by the need for nourishment and energy to fuel your performance, or are they motivated by emotional cravings and comfort? The answers may reveal areas where emotional eating might be hindering your leadership potential.

Which foods sharpen my mind, and which dull it?

- Consider how the foods you consume affect your mental clarity and focus. Are there certain foods that leave you feeling sluggish, distracted, or unfocused? Identify them and think about what changes can be made to prioritize foods that enhance cognitive function.

Could I lead at my highest level on my current diet?

- Evaluate if your current eating habits are supporting or limiting your ability to perform at your best. Are there gaps in your nutrition that could be addressed to enhance your physical energy, mental clarity, and overall resilience as a leader?

If my body is my vehicle, am I fueling it like a warrior or a victim?

- Think of your body as the vehicle that carries you through leadership challenges. Are you nourishing it to perform with strength and discipline, or are you feeding it in ways that leave you weak, tired, or unfocused? Reflect on how you can begin to fuel your body like a warrior, capable of facing any challenge head-on.

Practical Challenge

For today's challenge, track your meals and snacks throughout the day. When you feel the urge to snack, pause for 10 minutes before responding. During this pause, reflect on whether you're eating out of habit, hunger, or emotion. This practice allows you to break free from impulse-driven eating and move toward intentional choices.

Closing Visualization

Imagine two leaders six months from now. One indulges daily: heavy meals, sugar, alcohol. His body feels sluggish, his mind scattered, his leadership reactive. The other chooses a disciplined approach: he eats clean, fasts strategically, hydrates, and supplements wisely. His energy remains steady, his focus sharp, and his leadership magnetic. Which leader do you want to become?

The answer lies in every plate you build today. Each choice you make in fueling your body directly impacts your ability to lead with clarity and purpose.

Every bite you take is a decision — a choice between clarity and cloudiness, strength and weakness, discipline and indulgence. Nutrition is not just about personal health; it is about training yourself to lead effectively.

When you control your plate, you control your focus. When you master your diet, you master your days. Nutrition becomes the armor that fortifies your leadership. The warrior who fuels discipline into his body builds a fortress no craving can breach.

The Five-Day Fast: Training the Will Through Sacrifice

Why Fasting is More Than Diet

Fasting is often misunderstood as simply skipping meals to lose weight or detox. But in the context of leadership, it's much more than that. It's a practice of training both the mind and body to operate under deliberate self-control. It's a discipline that sharpens mental clarity, fortifies emotional resilience, and strengthens decision-making. When you deny your body its cravings, you reinforce your ability to lead with intention, instead of being swayed by impulsive desires.

Throughout history, fasting has been used by warriors, religious leaders, and high-performing executives to sharpen focus, increase patience, and build endurance. It's not about depriving the body, but about training it to operate without the immediate satisfaction of indulgence. The value of fasting lies in its power to teach control over impulse, which is essential for high-level leadership.

In today's fast-paced world, it's easy to be distracted by instant gratification. Whether it's food, social media, or any other short-term pleasure, these distractions can dilute your focus and weaken your ability to make thoughtful decisions. Fasting, however, allows you to resist these distractions. It teaches you that patience, restraint, and delayed gratification are not only necessary but powerful tools for a focused and successful leadership journey.

Every time you resist the urge to eat, you are reinforcing the discipline needed to resist temptations that don't align with your larger goals. Fasting becomes a microcosm for leadership, a practice where each moment of restraint contributes to long-term clarity, mental toughness, and focus. When you control your body's desires, you gain more control over your decisions, your team, and ultimately your destiny as a leader.

Fasting, when approached intentionally, does more than reset your body. It resets your leadership capacity. It teaches you that true leadership begins with self-discipline not from others' opinions, or external conditions but from within. In moments of pressure, whether in the boardroom, battlefield, or at home, a leader who can manage hunger, stress, and discomfort can make decisions with clarity and authority, instead of reacting impulsively to fleeting emotions.

Science Deep Dive – The Body's Transformation During Fasting

Fasting triggers a powerful biochemical transformation in your body, improving both physical and mental resilience. It's not just a matter of abstaining from food, it's a process that strengthens leadership qualities by enhancing clarity, focus, and emotional regulation.

1. Improved Insulin Sensitivity:

Within the first 24 hours of fasting, your body begins to improve insulin sensitivity. This means it can regulate blood sugar levels more efficiently, reducing the risk of insulin resistance. A well-functioning metabolic system allows for better energy management, ensuring your body isn't constantly driven by cravings or fluctuations in blood sugar.

2. Growth Hormone Surge:

By the time you reach 48–72 hours of fasting, growth hormone levels significantly increase. This hormone is responsible for preserving muscle mass and encouraging cellular repair. It's not only beneficial for physical health, but also for maintaining energy and focus during long, high-stakes days. Growth hormone helps the body adapt to the stress of fasting by supporting tissue recovery, ensuring that your body is as resilient as your mind.

3. Autophagy:

Autophagy, the body's natural process of "cellular cleanup," is activated during extended fasts. After 24-48 hours, your body begins to break down damaged or non-functional cells and recycle them into usable energy. This process helps maintain cellular integrity and eliminates the toxins that can affect mental and physical performance, leaving you feeling revitalized.

4. Hormonal Recalibration:

Fasting also recalibrates key hunger and satiety hormones. Ghrelin, the hormone responsible for stimulating hunger, spikes and falls in predictable waves. This teaches you that hunger is temporary and manageable. Leptin, the hormone that signals fullness, resets, allowing you to feel satiated with smaller portions. As a result, you're less driven by cravings and more in control of your eating habits.

5. Cortisol Stabilization:

Perhaps most importantly, fasting stabilizes cortisol, the stress hormone. This makes fasting a powerful tool for improving emotional regulation. When cortisol levels are steady, it's easier to maintain a calm, clear-headed approach to decision-making crucial for any leader facing high-pressure situations. Rather than reacting to stress impulsively, you're able to respond thoughtfully and with authority.

6. Mental Clarity with Ketones:

As the body shifts from burning glucose to ketones for energy, mental clarity improves. Ketones are a more efficient fuel for the brain, providing sustained energy for complex thinking and problem-solving. Leaders need mental sharpness in every situation, and the shift to ketone metabolism ensures that your focus remains sharp throughout the day.

Fasting in Leadership History

Historically, fasting has been more than just a form of self-denial; it has been an essential practice in leadership. Marcus Aurelius and other Stoic philosophers used to fast as a method of training their minds and proving their resilience. Their philosophy was grounded in the belief that a man who can master his own desires cannot be mastered by others. For the Stoics, fasting was a way to develop inner strength and demonstrate to themselves that they could endure discomfort without complaint, an essential quality for any leader.

In medieval times, knights preparing for battle would often fast before combat, seeing hunger as a means of purification. The act of fasting was a declaration of readiness, a demonstration that the body would not dictate their actions, especially in the high-stakes environment of warfare. Fasting symbolized a commitment to the higher mission of serving and protecting others, putting personal comforts aside for the sake of the greater good.

Even in modern times, military leaders have long understood the value of fasting or restricted rations. By practicing with limited resources, they sharpen mental toughness, resilience, and emotional control— qualities essential to leading effectively in high-pressure situations. These leaders prove that true strength isn't derived from indulgence, but from the ability to endure hardship, control impulses, and stay focused on the mission at hand.

Case Studies

Case 1: Religious Warriors – Fasting has long been used by spiritual leaders to sharpen focus and deepen their connection to a higher purpose. In many religious traditions, fasting serves as a practice to purify the body, strengthen discipline, and heighten spiritual awareness. These leaders understood that true power comes not from indulgence but from the ability to endure physical hunger for a greater, transcendent cause.

Case 2: Military Survival Training – In the military, soldiers are often trained under extreme conditions with limited rations. This practice builds grit, mental resilience, and the ability to maintain focus even when deprived of basic comforts. The discomfort experienced during survival training strengthens willpower, teaching soldiers that physical hunger or deprivation does not equate to weakness—it is an opportunity for growth and focus under pressure.

Case3: Modern Executives – High-performing executives and leaders often use extended fasting to reset both their physical and mental states. These leaders understand that fasting is more than just an act of depriving oneself; it is a practice that enhances clarity, patience, and mental toughness. By building the discipline to endure hunger, they improve their capacity to handle stress, focus on long-term goals, and make effective decisions, no matter the challenges they face.

Case 4: Modern Athletes – Elite fighters and endurance athletes frequently use controlled fasting to help cut weight, sharpen their mental discipline, and train their bodies to push through physical fatigue. In the competitive world of sports, fasting is not simply about survival or deprivation; it is about performance at the highest level. These athletes understand that by depriving their bodies of food for strategic periods, they are able to enhance their focus, improve recovery times, and push their limits further than most would ever believe possible.

The Five-Day Fast Protocol

Day 1: The Battle Begins

- On Day 1, hunger will be your greatest challenge. The cravings will rise sharply, and your body will demand attention. But this is the first test of your discipline. Your task is not to eliminate the hunger, but to watch it rise and fall without reacting. Hydrate, breathe, and acknowledge that this is just the beginning. The cravings are not permanent — they are waves, and your response to them is what will define your journey.

Day 2: The Mental Wall

- By Day 2, the body's energy dips. You'll feel irritable, fatigued, and mentally drained. This is the "wall" that many give up at. But pushing through this wall is where you learn the true strength of your willpower. This is where your mind can either take charge, or your body's demands can take control. The ability to stay committed to your goal and continue on this path will prove to you that the mind can overcome any weakness the body presents.

Day 3: Clarity Arrives

- By Day 3, ketones begin to rise, signaling the body's shift into a more efficient energy mode. Your hunger will subside, and mental clarity will begin to return. You'll experience a heightened sense of focus and energy as your brain shifts from relying on glucose to ketones as its primary fuel source. This day marks a significant turning point, and journaling becomes increasingly valuable as you process the thoughts and clarity that emerge.

Day 4: The Spiritual Shift

- By Day 4, hunger will be much less intense, and your body will feel lighter. Reflection deepens, and your mental clarity expands, helping you view challenges and problems from a new perspective. This is where the fast begins to transcend beyond physical endurance and turns into spiritual training. The discipline you're building manifests as strength in all areas of your life, including your leadership. You'll start to see the way forward with fresh eyes.

Day 5: Victory Over Flesh

- On Day 5, you reach the pinnacle of your fast: victory. This is the culmination of your efforts. You've not only withstood hunger, but you've trained your mind to dominate over cravings. You are sharper, calmer, and more disciplined. You've proven that control over the body leads to control over every aspect of your life. Fasting, at this point, becomes a declaration of self-mastery, and you emerge stronger for having faced and conquered the challenge.

Reflection Prompts

What cravings control me the most?

- Reflect on the cravings that have the most power over you. Are they emotional, physical, or social in nature? Identifying them will help you understand where your discipline needs the most attention.

How did hunger affect my focus and decisions?

- Think about the times when you felt hunger or discomfort during the fast. Did it affect your ability to focus or make decisions? How did you respond to these feelings, and what did that teach you about your limits and resilience?

Did I feel stronger or weaker when I denied my cravings?

- Consider the physical and mental effects of denying your cravings. Did you feel empowered, or was there a sense of weakness or frustration? This can help you better understand the impact of control and restraint on your leadership ability.

What lessons about leadership can I carry forward from fasting?

- Fasting is more than a physical challenge — it's a test of leadership. What lessons did you learn about self-discipline, decision-making, and managing discomfort that can improve your leadership style? How can these lessons be applied in your daily life and leadership?

Closing Reinforcement – Fasting as Modern Leadership

In today's world, where instant gratification and excess abound, fasting is a countercultural act. Yet it is precisely this countercultural nature that gives fasting its transformative power. The leader who chooses discipline over indulgence, who steps back from comfort to embrace sacrifice, earns respect in every area of life.

In business, fasting teaches clarity of thought and focus. It demonstrates the strength to resist distractions and make decisions rooted in purpose. In the military, it builds endurance, proving that mental toughness is as essential as physical strength. And in family life, fasting models' restraint, teaching those who look to you that discipline is the key to true freedom.

Fasting is a practice that transcends food; it is about learning to endure, to rise above, and to act with intention. When you fast, you are preparing not just your body, but your mind, for the challenges ahead. Each sacrifice becomes a step toward greater leadership, sharpening your clarity, focus, and resilience.

This is the essence of modern leadership the ability to lead with strength and purpose, even in the face of discomfort, knowing that every trial faced strengthens your resolve and sharpens your vision. Fasting, in its deepest sense, is a pathway to the ultimate freedom: the freedom to act decisively, to lead with confidence, and to influence the world with unshakable conviction.

A warrior who can endure five days of fasting proves that he is not a prisoner to the flesh. This sacrifice is not deprivation but a conscious, empowered choice. Every craving denied, every moment of discomfort faced head-on, sharpens your resolve and builds an inner strength that is unmatched.

Fasting is not just about abstaining from food, it's about building resilience. Each day spent fasting, each time you resist temptation, you train yourself to lead with clarity and purpose. The true power of leadership lies not in yielding to cravings but in mastering them.

Principle Takeaway: Across all contexts, fasting is not about abstinence for its own sake—it is a structured discipline to cultivate focus, resilience, and deliberate decision-making. Leaders who integrate controlled fasting into their routines demonstrate that mastery over self-precedes mastery over circumstances.

11

Your Personal Navigation System: Daily and Long-Term Application Plan

All the discipline, fasting, training, and emotional mastery in the world mean little if they are not anchored into a system that guides your life. A compass is only useful if it is used consistently. Leaders who master themselves for a season but drift without a plan often lose their way when distractions, temptations, and crises appear.

Your Personal Navigation System (PNS) is the framework that keeps you on course. Without it, discipline becomes random effort, scattered energy, and missed opportunities. With it, discipline becomes a predictable, purposeful force. This system transforms principles into practice, habits into progress, and vision into measurable outcomes. It is the difference between reacting to chaos and commanding your mission.

A navigation system anchors every decision, aligning your daily actions with long-term objectives. It integrates vision, principles, routines, reflection, and adaptability into one coherent framework.

Leaders who use such systems move deliberately, avoid drift, and build momentum toward legacy.

Core Elements of Your Personal Navigation System

Your personal navigation system translates mastery into action. Vision without structure drifts into chaos, and discipline without direction risks burnout. The system keeps you on course when distractions, temptations, and daily storms arrive, turning discipline into purpose.

Vision

Your vision defines the destination of your life and leadership. Without it, every decision is reactive. A clear, compelling vision gives you a north star that guides daily choices, helping you prioritize long-term objectives over fleeting comfort. Leaders who maintain focus on their vision make decisions decisively, even under pressure.

Principles

Principles act as guardrails that prevent deviation when challenges arise. They define the behaviors and standards you refuse to compromise, ensuring your actions align with your values. For example, a site lead might refuse to compromise safety protocols despite schedule pressures, demonstrating how principles anchor decisions in leadership integrity.

Habits

Habits are the daily actions that automate discipline. They are the autopilot of your navigation system, translating vision and principles into concrete routines. Anchored habits such as morning reflection, focused work blocks, and scheduled review periods ensure consistency and reduce the mental load of decision-making.

Reflection

Reflection provides feedback. By reviewing victories, setbacks, and choices, you gain insight into patterns that either support or hinder your navigation. Journaling, check-ins, and accountability practices allow leaders to recalibrate effectively, ensuring that short-term deviations do not compromise long-term objectives.

Adaptation

Even the most disciplined systems must remain flexible. Adaptation allows you to adjust course when disruptions occur without abandoning your destination. Leaders who can pivot while staying aligned to vision and principles maintain momentum, even in chaotic environments.

Science of Goal-Tracking

Understanding the science behind goal-tracking transforms discipline from theory into tangible progress. The human brain is wired to respond to clearly defined objectives. When you set structured goals and monitor progress, your brain releases dopamine, the neurotransmitter responsible for motivation and reward. Each completed milestone reinforces your effort, forming a positive feedback loop where progress generates momentum, focus, and a sense of achievement. Without structured tracking, this loop is vulnerable to distractions—social media, minor comforts, or trivial tasks—which fragment attention and dilute the impact of leadership.

Key Neuroscience Insights:

- Written Goals: Physically writing down objectives activates more neural pathways than verbal or mental intention alone. This makes your brain associate effort with measurable outcomes, increasing the likelihood of follow-through.
- Accountability: Declaring goals to a trusted peer, mentor, or team member enhances commitment. Your brain interprets these shared objectives as obligations rather than optional intentions, making you more likely to act decisively.
- Progress Feedback: Regularly reviewing performance, even in small increments, triggers dopamine spikes tied to achievement. This biochemical reinforcement encourages consistent action and strengthens neural pathways that support discipline.
- Cognitive Clarity: Tracking goals helps reduce mental noise. By externalizing tasks and priorities, your prefrontal cortex can focus on high-value actions rather than juggling multiple internal impulses.

Case Studies of Navigation

- Corporate Executives: Many leaders maintain a structured goal system, breaking long-term objectives into quarterly milestones. By reviewing progress weekly and adjusting course, they prevent drift and maintain focus on high-impact outcomes. Their navigation systems ensure that even during busy periods, decisions remain aligned with overarching vision.

- Project Leads: A project manager overseeing multiple teams uses daily check-ins and standardized templates to track progress. This allows rapid recalibration when unexpected issues arise, keeping the mission on track without overreliance on constant supervision.

- Site Supervisors: On complex operational sites, supervisors create simple, repeatable routines for team alignment. By embedding reflection and course correction into daily workflows, they maintain discipline, avoid errors, and achieve consistent results over time.

- Athletes & Performers: Elite performers structure training around measurable goals, journal progress, and adjust routines weekly. This disciplined approach creates long-term growth, demonstrating that small, intentional actions compounded over time produce significant outcomes.

The Daily Compass

Your day is a microcosm of your life. A disciplined leader structures each morning, midday, and evening to ensure alignment with vision, principles, and habits. Small, deliberate actions compound into lasting impact.

- Morning: Begin with silence, meditation, or reflection. Identify the top three priorities that will move you toward your vision. This focused start sets the tone for intentional leadership rather than reactive drift.

- Midday: Pause to assess your emotional and cognitive state. Are you acting with clarity and purpose, or are you drifting under stress? Short mental resets like a brief walk, controlled breathing, or reviewing your priorities help recalibrate focus.

- Evening: Reflect on the day. Ask yourself: What did I achieve? Where did I drift? Which habits or decisions strengthened my alignment, and which need adjustment? Evening reflection closes the loop, ensuring lessons are captured and applied.

The Weekly Map

- A week without intentional planning becomes a collection of unconnected days. Leaders who review, reflect, and plan weekly maintain momentum toward long-term goals while avoiding drift.
- Sunday Reset: Review the past week's actions, progress toward your vision, and adherence to principles. Identify patterns of success and areas needing adjustment. This prevents small misalignments from compounding over time.
- Weekly Plan: Define your top priorities for the upcoming week. Schedule tasks, align personal and professional goals, and anticipate potential distractions or challenges. Structured planning ensures energy is spent on what truly matters.
- Accountability: Share your weekly plan with a trusted ally, mentor, or peer. Accountability reinforces commitment, highlights blind spots, and fosters consistent execution.

Long-Term Path

Discipline only matters if it leads somewhere. Your long-term actions shape your trajectory, not just your daily victories. A navigation system ensures that each decision, habit, and reflection contribute to the life you are building.

- Quarterly Checkpoints: Every 90 days, review progress toward your vision. Assess which principles are consistently guiding decisions, which habits are reinforcing discipline, and whether any course corrections are necessary. Use this checkpoint to prune distractions and realign priorities.
- Annual Reset: Once a year, step away from routine to review your principles, reflect on your growth, and refine your goals. This annual recalibration strengthens foresight, ensuring your actions remain aligned with long-term objectives.
- Legacy Mindset: Consider the impact of your decisions beyond the immediate term. Ask yourself: What will my organization, team, or family inherit from the system I live by? Thinking in decades rather than days reinforces discipline and frames every choice as a building block toward enduring influence.

A leader who integrates long-term planning into daily and weekly practice ensures that short-term impulses do not derail the mission. Your navigation system becomes the framework that converts discipline into measurable outcomes, transforming intention into lasting impact.

Picture two leaders ten years from now. One drifts through days without structure, reacting to every distraction. Deadlines slip, priorities blur, and momentum fades. The other rises each morning with clarity: vision defined, principles intact, habits anchored, reflections logged, and adaptations made. Each choice compounds, building resilience, focus, and legacy.

Your personal navigation system turns discipline into destiny. It ensures every action; daily, weekly, quarterly aligns with your long-term purpose. Discipline without direction leads to burnout; direction without discipline drifts into mediocrity.

Unified Practical Challenge (30-Day Navigation Integration):

- Week 1: Define your vision and 3–5 non-negotiable principles. Write them down.
- Week 2: Establish three daily anchor habits that support your vision. Track adherence.
- Week 3: Begin nightly reflections. Log victories, lessons, and areas for improvement.
- Week 4: Create a quarterly review plan and simulate course correction for a past challenge.

By the end of 30 days, you won't just have habits, you will have a functioning compass for life. This challenge consolidates all chapter principles into one strong, actionable exercise exactly as per the buyer instruction. It reinforces vision, principles, habits, reflection, and adaptation without overwhelming the reader with multiple drills.

Key Takeaway: In every example, success stems not from raw talent or effort alone, but from a system that integrates vision, principles, habits, reflection, and adaptation. The leaders who excel are those who consistently apply their navigation framework, ensuring discipline translates into results.

www.ingramcontent.com/pod-product-compliance
Lightning Source LLC
Chambersburg PA
CBHW060419130626
46555CB00005B/2138